Also by Cathryn Grant

NOVELS
The Guest ◆ *Buried by Debt*
The Suburban Abyss ◆ *The Hallelujah Horror Show*
The Good Mother ◆ *Faceless* ◆ *An Affair With God*
She's Listening ◆ *The Good Neighbor*

THE ALEXANDRA MALLORY PSYCHOLOGICAL SUSPENSE
SERIES
The Woman In the Mirror ◆ *The Woman In the Water*
The Woman In the Painting ◆ *The Woman In the Window*
The Woman In the Bar ◆ *The Woman In the Bedroom*
The Woman In the Dark ◆ *The Woman In the Cellar*
The Woman In the Photograph ◆ *The Woman In the Storm*

THE HAUNTED SHIP TRILOGY
Alone On the Beach ◆ *Slipping Away From the Beach*
Haunting the Beach

NOVELLAS
Madison Keith Ghost Story Series ◆ *Chances Are*

SHORT FICTION
Reduction in Force ◆ *Maternal Instinct*
Flash Fiction For the Cocktail Hour
The 12 Days of Xmas

NONFICTION
Writing Is Murder: Motive, Means, and Opportunity

WRITING IS MURDER

Motive, Means, and Opportunity

*The Truth About Self-publishing And Why I'm
Glad I Did It*

Cathryn Grant

D2C

D2C Perspectives

PREFACE

What This Book Is

This is not a book about craft, there are plenty of those. This is not a book about discipline, although there will be some of that, inevitably. This is definitely not a book about marketing — at least not How TO Market, there is a seemingly infinite supply of those. Despite the title, and because I write crime fiction, this is absolutely not a book about writing crime fiction.

This is a book about angst. And quite a lot about murderous thoughts and feelings.

It's about keeping going no matter what.

It's about confidence, or lack thereof, in that ever elusive thing called "your voice".

It's about jealousy.

It's about frustration.

It's about finding a writing process that works and provides creative satisfaction.

It's about revision and polishing.

It's about flow.

It's about the reality that no one, NO ONE, knows why some books sell well and others do not.

It's about the ups and downs — the mountain peaks and the deep caverns of despair — wondering whether you'll ever find your audience.

It's about what worked for me in publishing and marketing and what didn't work. What still works, as of late 2018, despite a rapidly changing market. Some things never change — readers still want to get lost in other worlds, other lives.

It's about my journey from spending close to half a lifetime wanting to be published by a big-name New York publisher to deciding I would self-publish, and all that came after.

It's been a long and winding road.

Motive, Means, and Opportunity

In U.S. Criminal law, means, motive, and opportunity are the three aspects of a crime that must be established before guilt can be determined in a criminal proceeding. The terms refer to: the reason the individual felt the need to commit the crime (motive), the ability of the individual to commit the crime (means), and whether or not the individual had the chance to commit the crime (opportunity).

I write crime fiction. But I've always been less interested in means and opportunity, and obsessed with motive. My fiction is psychological and more about the perpetrators than those pursuing answers. Still, I often think about all three of those things.

It seemed natural to apply it to the fiction writing life.

Motive = Why do I want to be a writer?

Means = Craft and process and developing skill

Opportunity = Approximately 330 days a year, with a few holidays and family birthdays off, a bit of vacation, and the inevitable business of life.

Most of all the incredible opportunity to self-publish and all the benefits it offers to fiction writers, but also the struggle to change course when self-publishing was not anywhere on the horizon when you started writing.

Writing Is Murder…Why is writing murder and why did I choose this title? Because a writer has to suffocate her critical voice in order to get into the creative flow, stab her ego in the heart to get useful, honest feedback on her work, and drown her self-doubt in order to put her work out into the world.

Why Me?

Usually, books offering experience and inspiration to writers are written by those who have demonstrated success. Successful writers want to give back by helping those who come after them. They want to recount the paths they took to becoming full-time writers and best sellers and literary giants, letting their experience inspire and instruct.

When I wrote the first draft of this book, I wasn't that writer. I'm still not that writer. I'm not a best seller, and I'm certainly not a literary giant.

I delayed publishing this book because the experiences described here are still raw and were often difficult to write about. I doubted that a writer struggling to find an audience has anything to say.

I've had a long journey that veered wildly from unquenchable despair to near delusional optimism. It's taken over twenty years to get here. During those years, I've learned to tell a pretty good story, not that I'm brilliant at it or will ever stop working to improve.

At one time, I owned over 125 books on the craft and business of fiction writing! Not that bookshelves crammed with writing books demonstrate anything but a pathological need to learn everything I can about the craft and what it takes to succeed. I bought book after book looking for tips and secrets and most of all, constantly looking for a new collection of inspiring words that would keep me going in this sometimes lonely profession.

I've published a handful of short stories in the two most popular suspense magazines — Alfred Hitchcock and Ellery Queen Mystery Magazines. I've sold some flash fiction and had a few of those pieces anthologized. I received an honorable mention in the Zoetrope Magazine short fiction contest.

The rest, I've done without a publisher, with an ever- and sometimes stupidly- optimistic man by my side.

As of this writing, my husband and I have published twenty novels, twelve novellas, and a handful of short fiction collections. For the first five-and-a-half years of this venture, my sales were, well…that's a lot of what this book is about.

I'm writing about my experiences, my angst, lessons learned, my mistakes — hundreds of mistakes, possibly thousands — to encourage and support other writers who haven't yet found their audiences. I'm writing about my decision and my protracted *in*decision over self-publishing in order to help other writers who are wrestling with the choice between pursuing a traditional publisher or going it alone.

If you think about self-publishing but view it as the antithesis of your dreams, this book is for you.

And I'm writing to help those who have been self-publishing for months or years and are discouraged, especially in the face of thousands of success stories.

I hope it will make the isolated life of a fiction writer a little less isolated. I hope it will talk you off the ledge when you find yourself out there, staring into the abyss.

Final Introduction

This book was conceived in 2013 over a breakfast of veggie scramble, hash browns, and dark roast coffee on a Sunday morning after I whined to my husband for the ten-thousandth time — *Why do I keep wasting my writing time?*

That Sunday breakfast followed a horrible Saturday. At that time, I lived for Saturdays.

Saturday was the day I got to experience my dream of being a full-time writer. I had ten glorious hours to take a long walk and think about the next scenes in my novel, to give solid attention to my story, to write fiction for at least six of those hours. I had the freedom to take a glorious ninety-minute lunch break, eating leftover Chinese garlic prawns and spicy green beans while burying myself in a novel or a book about the craft of fiction.

That Saturday, not for the first time, I'd wasted over four of those precious hours. Despite the blue California sky, it had become a desperately gloomy day. I was two years into self-publishing, without any traction in sales of my three published novels. I was frustrated. Alongside my three novels, I had a series with seven novellas as well as several collections of flash fiction.

Rather than writing, I often spent Saturdays sinking

into the hive mind of the indie publishing world — KBoards (formerly Kindle Boards) and Joe Konrath's blog and the hundreds of discussion comments, all sharing experiences and expertise. Some comments were as gloomy as my frame of mind, some were filled with squeals of delight over what seemed like instant sales success.

I rationalized this wallowing in online discussions because I was hanging out with fiction writers.

Among many other posts on KBoards that day, I read about a writer who was selling fifty copies of his short story a month at $2.88 for a single story!!! Most of my short fiction collections, priced at $.99, hadn't sold fifty copies in their lifetimes.

Why? Why? Why? Alone in my writing space, I cried and raged. *Why can't that be me? Why isn't that me?*

Maybe I'm not very good!?

But, but, but…my traditionally published short stories. My acclaimed flash fiction. Maybe I'm just not a very good novelist? Maybe no one wants to buy flash fiction (true, to some extent)? Maybe…?

There was no real answer. Marketing blah blah, genre blah blah blah. Professional covers. Blurbs. Twitter. Reviews. Bundles. Cross-promoting. All of those topics will work their way into this book. But then, there was no answer. The fact was that this guy was selling a lot of books — short stories, the kind of fiction that "everyone" knows don't sell much — I was not.

I am a very private and proud person. Intensely aware of my flaws and failures but very unwilling to expose them (as if by keeping my mouth shut, no one will notice my flaws!)

Even with people close to me but especially in public, which is why I was an utter failure at blogging. Self-revelation is an important part of blogging, and from that perspective, writing this book is the most difficult thing I've ever done. But I feel driven to write it anyway. I started it in a burst of enthusiasm, then put it aside. I re-started it and cut out all of the self-revelation. I put it aside. I started again and put the personal stories back in. This year I started it and abandoned it twice during a single week in the Spring, once in Summer, and once in the Fall, before this, hopefully final, attempt.

But I hope that by telling the brutal truth of my experiences and my pettiness and neurotic self-analysis and frustration and utter financial terror, I'll help someone else. Even just one writer trying to find a path to being a self-supporting fiction writer. Even one writer trying to decide whether self-publishing is a viable path for her, or him.

On April 30, 2012, I was thrilled that I'd finally managed

to go two weeks without cheating.

In our marriage, cheating had become the way I told my husband I'd failed for the hundredth in my effort to not obsessively check book sales at the various ebook stores.

I knew it wasn't healthy to be looking at book sales multiples times a day, and by multiple I mean sometimes hourly. It's difficult when so much data is available at the click of a computer key. Just a little peek to see if someone else bought a book. Just this once…

It gave us a bit of a laugh when I texted him: *I cheated.* A sad little emoji sat beside the words.

Then came my follow-up message: *But guess what! I sold a book!! I sold two books. I had four free downloads.*

He always forgave the cheating. He was as thrilled as I was.

Less thrilling was when my friends at work asked me how book sales were going. The vice-president of the organization where I worked was fond of saying that if what you say is fifty-one percent truthful, it's the truth. (That's the corporate world I couldn't wait to escape from.) I didn't want to lie to my friends, but I wrapped my answer in layers of vagueness — *Up and down. Improving. Not where I want them to be yet.* I thought they wouldn't guess that sales were so dismal a single book sent me into shrieks of elation.

On that memorable April 30th, I was grouchy from my day job and anxious for my husband to get home. To avoid cheating, we'd committed to only checking sales together. We were a team! I couldn't check without him, but sad to say, I'd already cheated earlier in the day — we'd sold a copy of my first novel on Barnes & Noble.

The thrill! Someone found my book! They paid money for it! And not just 99 cents!

Through my cheating, I also knew I'd sold a few flash fiction collections and a novella in my ghost story series.

Then, as we looked together, more thrills awaited. One copy of my second novel had sold on Amazon!! And that didn't include the record of the sale of the novel I bought myself because I was so depressed that the rank in the Amazon store had sunk below 1,000,000. And, I'd sold three more novellas and a short story collection, and two more volumes of flash fiction!

It was amazing! Unbelievable! Magical!

I'd done nothing — no tweeting, interviews, blogging, Facebook-ing, seeking reviewers. My simple marketing technique of novel samples in the back of 99-cent short fiction collections seemed to be paying off.

People were reading my introductory books and coming back for more! And then, it didn't pay off. My short fiction sank to oblivion, and my novels gasped to keep their heads above water.

There I sat, five years later. That "brilliant" marketing technique of excerpts no longer worked. At all. In the spring of 2017, I'd sold a lot more books, I'd had days of twenty to fifty sales, but they were spikes. Sales fluctuated wildly, mostly down.

Why would anyone put herself through this? You need a big publisher to market your books. It's impossible to stand out in the crowd, rise above the noise, get attention without that professional marketing push from a corporation with clout. I looked in the mirror — *Are you insane?*

Possibly, I am. I also tend toward pessimism, but despite that, am strangely, blindly persistent.

If you think there might be a reason why I persisted to the point of madness, if you're wondering whether self-publishing is the right path for you, I have a lot to say.

More than anything, I want to pay it forward. Bloggers who virtually yelled at me to quit whining and demanded to know why I wasn't spending the majority of my free time writing, inspired me. Bloggers who told me what I needed to hear over and over and *over* again, inspired me. Books that taught me about craft and the industry and marketing, and the long, slow effort to find discipline and a voice and wrestle ninety thousand words into a story, with life-like characters battling their demons and other human beings, inspired me.

I hope I can do the same for you. I hope I can let go of my intense privacy and be open and raw and let you see inside the life and mind of one writer.

If you've ever had a neurotic thought about your fiction writing or the realities of the publishing industry, this book is for you.

So there you have it, a book with four introductions!

BACKSTORY

I Want To Be A Writer

When I was in fourth grade, I decided I wanted to be a fiction writer. I promptly wrote a novel titled, *The Mystery of the Missing Mansion*.

Just as promptly, my mother typed it up, made a cover out of cardboard covered with contact paper, and voila — I was a published writer!

I have no idea what made me decide I wanted to write fiction. I loved reading, and possibly I had the impression that being a writer meant I could bury myself in fiction all day long. Maybe I was influenced by Jo March — the writer in *Little Women* who first inspired countless female writers. I loved the images of her scribbling on her stack of papers in a tiny attic room.

When I was in fifth grade, I learned to put paperback novels inside my textbooks and stand the textbooks up on the desk to look as if I was studying history or science or whatever other topic was contained in that oversized, dreadfully heavy book.

At home, I spent hours on a large living room chair, my legs tucked up, reading. Once, when I was reading *Airport* by Arthur Hailey, my mother called me to set the table. I ignored her. She called several more times, finally demanding that I get my nose out of my book. Never.

I loved mysteries most of all, which explains why a mystery was my first fiction writing effort. Since my book told the story of four children discovering an abandoned house which then disappears, it contained an element of magical realism. I liked the not-knowing that mysteries provided, the slow revelation of truth. I gobbled up my Grandmother's copies of the Judy Bolton series featuring an amateur sleuth. I also read some Nancy Drew, but I liked Judy better. She wasn't so perfect and polite. I read Erle Stanley Gardner and Agatha Christie.

I sat beside my father and watched *The FBI* TV show, gripped by the enactment and investigation of major crimes, especially murder. It was the stories of personalized murder, kidnapping, and other crimes of passion that ate their way into my bloodstream. When *The FBI* went off the air, we watched *Hawaii Five-O*.

When I was older I watched *Murder She Wrote*, the *Perry Mason* films, and *Columbo*. I watched re-runs of the old black and white *Perry Mason* TV series. Even today, I can't get enough of *Dexter, True Detective, The Killing, The Shield*, and even *House of Cards*, which at its heart is a noir-ish tale of betrayal and crime. The list goes on.

As a child, I recorded my thoughts in small, locked diaries. When my sister read one of my diaries, I stopped writing, for a while. Ultimately, I couldn't be stopped. Although I was certainly sidetracked many times for many different reasons.

Somewhere along the way, I forgot about wanting to be a writer. In the book, *Reviving Ophelia*, it's suggested that girls often lose their true selves around the age of ten. Mary Pipher, a psychologist, observes that coming of age in a media-saturated culture preoccupied with unrealistic ideals of beauty causes "girls to become 'female impersonators' who fit their whole selves into small, crowded spaces." Many lose spark, interest, and even IQ points as a "girl-poisoning" society forces a choice between being shunned for staying true to oneself and struggling to stay within a narrow definition of female.

That's changed to some extent since I came of age, but not as much as we'd like to think.

I know I was diverted from my attempts to write fiction when I had my first mad crush at the age of nine, followed by another crush that consumed me for nearly four years. I played the clarinet, carrying it back and forth to school twice a week in a black case. Early during fifth grade, a new boy came to our school. He had blonde hair and blue eyes and carried a clarinet in a coffee-with-cream-colored case. All I thought about was that boy and band practice and sitting side by side in our metal folding chairs.

In high school, there were more boys to consume my thoughts. Then rock 'n roll, school dances, homework, sleepovers, the beach, a boyfriend who didn't exist solely in my imagination. Through it all, I kept reading, but I didn't write at all.

My love of writing fiction was displaced by my love of the opposite sex.

By college, I'd decided I wanted to be a visual artist. I spent the first year buying art supplies and failing to achieve anything that showed even a spark of talent. I changed majors three times and eventually graduated with a BA in History, simply relieved to be finished.

Before I finished my last year of college, I fell in love and married a Lutheran minister. Then I was off to a dull job at IBM, first answering phones in a call center, then working in electronic supplies inventory control, and finally editing technical papers. Slightly adrift, it never occurred to me to think about what I might do with a degree in history. It was a subject I enjoyed and allowed me to graduate.

While I sat at a desk, bored to tears, answering phones for twenty men, my mother reminded me — *Remember how you wanted to be a writer? Maybe you can write when you're bored at work.*

I bought a steno pad and started writing when I could. Mostly journals. Despite all those years of reading, I wasn't really sure how to write fiction. But I wrote. Finally, I decided to take a night class in fiction writing at our local junior college.

Only one story stands out from that class, possibly we just wrote a single story during the semester. My story was based on my experience of getting lost in the forest at Yosemite National Park when I was eight years old. I wrote about my parents' effort to encourage independence and self-reliance by sending me off to the restroom alone, a short walk from our picnic spot. I have absolutely no sense of direction, which they didn't yet realize, and clearly, not a lot of logic at that age because when I walked out of the restroom, instead of looping back around to the other side as I'd done when I arrived, I walked straight.

It was several minutes before I realized I should have been nearing the picnic area. Everything looked the same but different — the same trees, the same ground covering of dead leaves and pine needles. I crossed a shallow dip like a dried riverbed. I didn't remember that, but I kept walking, slowly understanding that something was wrong. I turned back, now with a distorted sense of where I was, surrounded by trees on all sides, not a building, a road, a trail, or a human being in sight.

Soon, I was running, crying. I tried to make myself stop, tried to think which way to turn, but I had no idea. By some stroke of luck, after wandering for about two hours, I found a road. I began walking and more luck, or maybe a deeply imbedded, unconscious sense of direction that was sharper than evidence seems to suggest, I saw signs that named familiar places. The name of a waterfall. Our camping area. I made my way to our campground and the centrally located water pump. I was able to orient my direction from the pump to our tent cabin, a physical memory after days of walking back and forth to that pump.

A while later, my frantic family returned to find me sitting at the picnic table filling the outlines in my coloring book.

According to my parents, I'd been missing for three, horrifying hours.

This was the story I submitted to my class — a lightly fictionalized memory of the experience. One line of the story referred to the trees that *loomed* over me. The instructor wrote in the margin of my manuscript — *loom-loom, loom, loom, loom* with the ominous cadence of threatening background music in a film. I felt trite and clichéd and foolish for thinking I could write anything interesting or compelling. By then, I was pregnant with my first child. I skipped the final class and received an incomplete.

Still, the desire refuses to die.

Our local paper announces a Christmas-themed short story contest. I dash off a story about a newly married woman whose minister husband brings a homeless, pregnant teenager to Christmas dinner. I receive second place, my story appears in the newspaper, and I win a dinner at a local Chinese restaurant. My story…in the newspaper!

I'm hooked. People might want to read what I write after all.

Fast forward three years.

I'm writing short stories and getting them published in religious-themed periodicals. My marriage and social life are consumed by the church. My mothering is under the scrutiny of fifty or sixty middle-aged and elderly women bursting with parenting advice. Because of that environment, my stories are all about people discovering they're not living according to the principles of the Bible. But I'm publishing them…and I'm getting paid!

Fast forward again.

I'm working part-time, in a church, of course. The minister writes a weekly column for the town paper.

If he can write a column about his random thoughts regarding life and social issues, so can I.

My town paper accepts my proposal, and I spend the next two years writing a slice-of-life column about the suburbs, mothering two small children, and the humorous moments of marriage. And I'm getting paid!

While I'm writing cheerful stories, my marriage is in a downward spiral of emotional abuse, harsh directives from "god", and mounting credit card debt. I'm living in a house co-owned by the church, driving a car given to us by a church member, and sending my youngest daughter to the church pre-school. I have no one to talk to about my struggles because all my friends are essentially my husband's employer. Through it all, I keep writing and writing and writing. And reading. I read theological books and am eaten with guilt. I read religious fiction and despair over my weak faith. I read religious parenting books and am terrified of every wrong word and lax decision and the eternal impact on my daughters.

I'm referred to a Christian counselor. I try to talk to her about my marriage, and she advises me to yield my soul and my will to my husband. I confess that I really want to write fiction, but feel guilty because good fiction involves conflict and maybe God will be pissed off if I thrill over conflict. The longing to write crime stories is a distant memory. She advises me to write about abortion. She emotes about what a crime it is, and how it's such a terrible thing and insists that this is what I should be writing about.

I don't go back.

When my husband assaults me in our living room, tries to strangle me, and pushes me to the floor, and all I can do is whisper that he needs to be quiet so our children don't hear, I'm disgusted with myself.

With lots of support from my family, I visit a lawyer and file for divorce. (A thousand times not so quick and easy as it sounds, but I'm trying to stay focused on how writing fiction wove its way through every part of my life.)

My upbeat column titled *Moments to Savor*, filled with domestic humor, is no longer viable. I get a brief internship with the same weekly paper and write personality profiles for a while. Once again, I'm getting paid! But it's coffee and movie money. I get an administrative job in high tech. Then, I marry the love of my life, and together we start shepherding my children through high school.

Yes, I'm sidetracked, but in a very nice way.

One day, I'm talking to a few co-workers, and they'd considering returning to school to get their MBAs. I know an MBA would be my ticket out of clerical work. I look at the requirements for an MBA program and discover there are a few qualifying classes I missed during college. I calculate two years taking night classes, then starting the MBA, more night school for approximately three years. By then, my children will be grown. I'll be gone from home two nights a week, and on the weekends, I'll be doing homework.

Like waking from a stupor, it occurs to me — *What if I put those same hours into launching a writing career?* I can get up before dawn and write. I can do it all! Work full time, be a mom and write fiction. Sounds much easier than night classes and homework. And a lot more fun.

Despite my failure to pursue an MBA, I manage to make the giant leap out of clerical work to become a web manager and then a competitive analyst. My job gets more demanding, but my salary goes up and all those sleepless nights when I wondered how I'd put my daughters through college dissolve. Best of all, I'm managing to get up an hour before I need to get ready for work to write fiction.

On My Way

The first full-length project I tackled was a heavily autobiographical mainstream novel. Well, I didn't start out with an intention to make it autobiographical, but like nearly all first novels, that's what it morphed into. I can't remember how long it took to write and I have no idea what happened to the manuscript. I only vaguely remember the story. When I typed *The End* I was thrilled to know I could write 100,000 words and kinda sorta make them hang together and kinda sorta have a plot, maybe. There was conflict, I remember that!

I wrote more short stories, but they were darker than what I'd written in the past. The religious markets that published my stories when I was the preacher's wife were no longer a good fit. I didn't need a rejection letter to tell me that.

In 2000, my sister got married in Hawaii. When we returned to California, I longed to carry that island paradise calm into the rest of my life. It occurred to me there was one small corner of my life where I could infuse more calm on a consistent basis. Listening to audio novels would take my mind off traffic snarls and bad drivers (not me, of course, just all the other drivers who do stupid things), and increase my equanimity.

At the public library, I stumbled across an audiobook of Ruth Rendell's, *The Bridesmaid*.

I devoured it.

It's a dark story of a young man and his infatuation with a

mysterious and seductive woman. He begins a relationship with her and becomes obsessed. That obsession leads him on a twisted journey.

When I finished that book, I knew without a doubt the kind of stories I wanted to write. Crime fiction, sure. The mysteries I grew up with, not so much. I longed to tell stories that were dark and more sinister than the typical solving of a crime. I was still interested in *whodunnit*, but I was far more interested in the *why*.

With this new mindset and more clarity into the type of stories I love, I wrote a short story titled, *Peace on Coolidge Drive*. I mailed it off to Ellery Queen's Mystery Magazine. In January 2001 I received a phone call from the assistant editor. She wanted to know whether I'd published stories in any other nationally recognized magazines. If not, I qualified for their Department of First Stories. They sent me a check, and I framed the magazine cover where my name appeared.

I was on my way.

That was seventeen years ago. Not quite as *on-my-way* as I thought at the time, more of a snail on her way across rough terrain.

Next, I dove into a 125,000-word psychological suspense novel. I sent it to agents and received form rejections. I took it to a writer's conference and received good feedback from a published writer who read the first chapter. I sent it to more agents and was rewarded with more form rejections.

Meanwhile, I read a lot of books — about writing, about finding agents, about publishers, about the market. I learned that 125,000 words were inadvisable for a first-time novelist — *Aim for 90,000, I was told*.

I wrote more short stories and two years later, published *Cirque du Bohemia* in Ellery Queen. Two years. This was taking forever.

I worked, I raised my daughters, I started playing golf with my husband.

Every morning I got up at five o'clock to write for an hour before I started the day. After a while, I decided an hour wasn't enough time. I'd settle down, and with my mental distractions, sometimes eked out only a few hundred words. Other days, the screen remained blank.

I managed to convince my husband to get up and make coffee for me at four a.m. I relished my newly-expanded writing time. Two hours! My daughters teased me when I fell asleep on the couch at eight in the evening.

Discouraged from the lack of interest in my novel, anxious to quit my day job and become a full-time fiction writer, all my industry and market studying educated me on the fact that fifty percent of the fiction market was romance novels. I would become a romance writer. I'd never read a romance novel. I had the impression they were easy to write, they were shorter than the novels I usually read, and I could tell a story, couldn't I? A romance was a story.

I bought a few books on writing romances and about thirty Silhouette and Harlequin romance novels. I read them all and plunged in. I wrote my first romance, sent a query and a few chapters off to Silhouette. I received a request for the full manuscript. I was elated. Except...by then, a year had passed. I looked at my life — my husband, my daughters, my job, my two hours to write each day, with a few hoarded hours on Saturdays.

Did I want to spend those precious hours writing stories I didn't have an affinity for? Request for a full manuscript or not?

The answer, and I still remember the date because I wrote it in my journal — Leap Day — February 29, 2004 — was, no.

Slightly disoriented from writing something that didn't fit, or maybe a realization that I needed to step back from trying so hard to get published, I decided to spend the next year writing short stories. I'd see how many short stories I could produce. I'd work on finding my voice, learning more about story-telling, and most of all, write whatever I pleased. I ended the year with about fifteen or twenty stories. Not too bad. I revised and submitted some that I thought had potential. None of them were accepted.

In 2005 I started another novel. In the end, it would take me five years to get that novel to a place where I thought I was ready to pursue an agent. I continued submitting short stories. I started to follow the rules to get to publication. At the time, the rules were:

1. Publish short fiction to prove to agents you can write publishable fiction
2. Learn to write a query letter
3. Research agents. This was a lot of work, with sub-rules: find out what types of books they represent, find other writers who are agented by them, read those writers' books, and if possible, be prepared to tell agents why you liked those books and therefore why s/he would be a good fit for your book.
4. Rewrite your book
5. Get critical feedback on your book
6. Revise your book.
7. Query agents.

The novel I stared in 2005 was prompted by a line that seemed to come out of the ether, and lodged in my brain like a strand of celery between my molars — "That woman's not wearing a bra."

In part, it was born from years of listening to women judge each other — *Why did she dye her hair? Why doesn't she dye her hair? She looks ridiculous in that outfit, she should stop trying to be a teenager. She doesn't discipline her kids. She works too much, so her kids are brats. She stays home and does nothing all day…*And on and on it goes. My writer's brain saw a group of women sitting around a picnic table, waiting for their kids to get out of school. A woman who is younger, more attractive, and dresses unconventionally walks across the playground. It turns out she's a single mother, and the other women all react, some violently, to her unsettling presence and the subtle threat to their marriages.

That line stuck in my head and drove me to start thinking about who these women were.

I worked on backstory and notes for several months and then I started writing. I wrote the novel. I re-wrote the novel. I wrote it again.

I realized that the previous novels had been practice. Now I sort of knew what I was doing. I'd been dabbling enough. Now I was going to write a psychological suspense novel. I was going to craft it into something "good enough" to take to an agent and launch my writing career. The detour into romance had provided good lessons in plot structure, pacing, and dialog. The autobiographical novel felt like something I'd needed to get off my chest. It had taught me that I had the discipline to write nearly every day, carrying a 100,00-word story to the end.

While this was going on, I was getting more responsibility in my day job. The hours were long, and some mornings I was too tired to write. Or I got up to write and worked myself into a frenzy of worrying about the quality of the writing, the plot, the dialog more than I actually put words on the screen. I worked on the novel for about two years and started to feel it might be kind of good. At the same time, I submitted stories here and there and collected a few more rejection letters.

While I was re-writing, I went to a one-day writer's conference. One of the lectures I attended was given by a local author. Rather than talking about plot or structure or character, rather than talking about finding time to write or any of the hundred other things discussed at writers' conferences, she spoke for a few minutes about the writing life, then she said — *We're going to write.*

She told us to take out a notebook and pen and assigned an exercise to the room full of fifty or sixty writers. I wrote for the allotted ten or fifteen minutes. She made us write! That was impressive, sadly. It wasn't something that was done at writers' conferences I attended in the past. Instead of talking about writing, we were actually writing. It was a lesson in what matters, but I don't think I fully realized that at the time.

When I learned that she taught writing classes in her home, I was in. I took her card, went to her website, and signed up for a not-inexpensive twelve-week class.

A year later, a classmate in one of those classes encouraged me to submit one of my short stories to the Zoetrope Magazine short fiction contest. I'd never heard of the magazine and am not sure why she suggested that one, but I followed her advice.

The day the email arrived giving the results, I was working late, frustrated at many, many re-dos of some market analysis. It was my birthday, and I'd hoped to leave work early, which was making me even more irritable. When I opened the email and saw that out of 2500 entrants I'd received one of ten honorable mentions, I cried. I thought — *This is it. This time, I'm really on my way. Nothing will stop me now. Agents will fall all over me.*

A Fork In the Road

In the fall of 2009, I decreed my novel done. I was ready to seek representation by an agent, confident I'd find one who would lead me to a publishing contract with one of the Big Six. Yes, Big Six at that time, alongside big dreams in my head.

In researching agents as the lead-up to the query gauntlet, I'd learned that a "platform" was required to generate publisher interest. A platform basically means a group of people who will be inclined to buy your book once it's published. I'd already been blogging for a few months and had developed a small community of other writers. I'd published four short stories. Although that didn't really qualify as a platform, it met one of the "rules" laid down by agents. I even had that honorable mention from a literary magazine. Surely, I had all the keys to generate agent interest.

Realizing that the requirement for a platform extended to social media, I launched a Twitter account. I madly sought followers, mostly by following writers. It was fun and supportive, although a little stressful trying to figure out how to be witty online. The idea of spitting out what was running through my mind or my life at any moment in time seemed slightly self-conscious and forced. I read books on how to tweet effectively. I mostly tweeted about writing and replied and retweeted to other tweets about writing.

I loved Twitter. I still do. Or at least the idea of Twitter. When I exchanged thoughts with people in Australia and Ireland and the UK, I was mesmerized by the idea that I could meet people all over the world without any barriers. People I would never in a hundred years meet in the physical world.

Even more than the potential for new and interesting relationships, I was thrilled with Twitter in particular and the online world in general. It seemed custom-made for introverts. I could socialize when I felt like it. I could moderate the noise and frenzy with curated lists. I could step away to re-energize by simply closing a browser or an app. I didn't have to feel trapped in a room with too much noise, too many conversations, too many personalities that left no room for genuine one-on-one conversation. It was heaven, until it turned to hell.

The noise on social media is incessant. It's not so introvert-friendly after all. The number of people to juggle is overwhelming. The need to think fast on my feet is the same. Maybe it's the introvert thing, maybe I'm just not that clever, but when I do locate a shred of wit, it's usually four hours after the fact, just like I do after face-to-face gatherings. An introvert is an introvert even when she's in a room by herself staring at her feed.

None of this was even remotely close to a platform that would interest a publisher, but this was the early days of telling fiction writers they needed a platform as non-fiction writers had known for years. The demand for a platform hadn't yet grown to mammoth proportions. It was basically another word for an online presence. Surely my online presence was adequate. The book was what mattered, right?

One afternoon I saw a tweet announcing that a fairly well-known and respected literary agent was going to be at a very small mystery writers' conference fifty miles from my home. It was held in a beautiful old hotel — The Claremont in Berkeley. They could only accommodate twenty-five people, and there were still open slots. I signed up.

My husband and I drove to Berkeley and had a scrumptious dinner. For the rest of the weekend, he would hang out in our charming room reminiscent of the early decades of the twentieth century, with windows that actually opened, letting in the blue autumn sky and fresh air.

Twenty-five mystery writers gathered in a room with floor-to-ceiling windows overlooking a garden, and French doors opening to the rest of the hotel.

On the first morning, we were given the opportunity to read to the group the opening paragraphs of a work in progress. The published writers who were hosting the event and the agent would provide feedback on the what we'd read. When my turn came, I read with an eerily calm voice, starting with my provocative line of dialog — "That woman's not wearing a bra." The scene went on to describe a single mother sauntering across an elementary school playground, the reactions of the woman threatened by her overt sexuality, and their initial encounter. But I didn't get to the initial encounter.

Before I'd finished the second paragraph, one of the published writers said in an authoritative tone, "Where's the murder? This is a *mystery* writers' conference."

I explained that this was psychological suspense. That it was a story that built slowly from seemingly normal circumstances into an atmosphere of anxiety and dread, culminating in violence. My novel exposed *why* the crime occurred, not the uncovering of clues and evidence.

That satisfied her, sort of. I continued reading.

When I was finished, I was told my story was intriguing. Whatever else was said flew out of my head. The others seemed unfamiliar with psychological suspense as I knew it, the psychological suspense of British novels and films — the stories of Ruth Rendell. Maybe it explained why another favorite psychological suspense writer, Patricia Highsmith, spent most of her career living and writing in Europe. My work didn't seem to fit into a category. Or maybe it just didn't fit the American market. In the publishing industry, everything has to fit. There's little room for misfits, even though writers, as a rule, tend toward the misfit end of the spectrum. Only in literary fiction does there seem to be a welcoming of the unconventional. But this was before I learned something that should have been glaringly obvious. Publishing is a business. It's about sales and marketing and return on investment. It's about minimizing risk and target audiences. Those things require a well-defined product. But I'll get to that later.

During the morning break, I ran up to my room and dumped all my angst on my husband. He spoon-fed me some reassurance. I trotted back down with a confident mask plastered across my face.

After the break, still feeling somewhat wobbly, trying to shake off the suggestion that my novel and I didn't belong there, I took my seat.

The glamorous New York agent came in from the garden. She called across the room to me, "Cathryn! I was standing outside, and I put my hand across my brow to block the sun, and my diamond ring glittered — just like Amy's!"

I melted with pleasure. An agent remembered my line! Surely that meant…something!

There was hope. I was a good writer. I would absolutely find an agent. Maybe even this agent would represent me. Later that weekend she said she was looking for literary crime fiction. Was I literary? I had no idea. I certainly wasn't mystery, that had been pointed out quite clearly. I certainly wasn't a thriller writer, or not really, or maybe. I was a writer without a genre — a misfit.

That evening, several of the other not-yet-published writers reassured me that they enjoyed my story. They told me they felt bad for me and that I handled it well. I relaxed — a little. Even one of the published writers, a goddess who had crossed that golden threshold, said she'd enjoyed my writing. Surely that meant…something.

After critique group feedback designed to "make it better", I was starving for feedback that I could write. It had been years now. Could I write a novel or not?

The next morning, we had a chance to try out our pitch by reading our query letters to a few of the published writers. They would listen and give advice. I gave my pitch, and it was discussed. I've forgotten what they said, but the subject of my non-genre came up. One writer said, "You could call it Suburban Noir."

A chime went off in my head. Suburban. That fit! That definitely fit. I wasn't sure I knew a lot about Noir, but the suburbs! I was a suburban girl if nothing else. I moved to the Santa Clara Valley when I was six years old. I lived in a ranch-style house with a swimming pool. I attended a suburban junior college. I'd lived all my adult life in the suburbs, and my children attended suburban schools. Heck, the title of my novel was *The Demise of the Soccer Moms.* Suburbia was in my blood.

Despite a pleasant and relatively untroubled childhood, I'd managed to develop a dark view of the suburbs. Even as a child, I felt the cookie-cutter, keep-up-appearances, the competitive cooking and child rearing and home decorating that simmered below the surface. The potential for violence and "inappropriate" sex. All of that sounded very Noir to me.

On Sunday afternoon we had a Q&A with the agent. I asked whether it was true what I'd heard — that my multi-year effort to publish short stories had been worthwhile, that those credits would help capture an agent's attention. She said, "Absolutely. It shows you can string the twenty-six letters of the alphabet together in a way that someone besides your mother, your aunt, your sister wants to read." I glowed. I had a memorable story. I had credentials. Finding an agent would be easy.

Despite the rough start to the weekend, I walked away with a focus and another tiny piece of confidence that I was ready. It was time to start querying agents.

In January of 2010, with a manuscript polished until it gleamed, my small list of short story credits, a little over eleven-hundred Twitter followers in hand, a blog about writing, and another blog where I posted flash fiction, I started the search.

Only nine emails into my list of thirty carefully vetted agents to query, I had a bite! A junior agent said my writing was good and the story intriguing. She asked me to send the full manuscript. I danced. I cheered. I tweeted. I told everyone I knew — *An agent wants to read my book! She thinks my writing is good!!*

Three weeks later a brief email came back from the senior agent — *The writing is good, but I'm not passionate enough about this book to take it on.*

Slowly, over the next two years, I would come to understand that "not passionate enough" meant she didn't think she could sell it to one of the editors she worked with. I learned what should have been obvious from the start — agents are saleswomen. They do not have a legal background and therefore can't give solid advice on contracts. For the most part, they don't negotiate much beyond minor contractual changes. They take on books they like, that they know they can sell.

They're "passionate" about books they know fit solidly into a particular genre, or can be marketed as breakout or blockbuster bestsellers. They seek books that will make them money, obviously. And that's fair. That fifteen percent commission is their livelihood. But a rejection by an agent says **absolutely nothing** about the quality of your writing, and possibly not even their interest in your story (if they don't know how to sell it), or even the market potential for that book. It says everything about what that agent has sold herself or what's doing well in the marketplace.

But I didn't know that. I inferred that my book was not one that generated passion. Still, I continued querying, reminding myself that personal taste surely played into this. I received form letter rejections — *Not right for us, good luck placing it elsewhere.*

The agent who compared the refracted sunlight in her diamond ring to my protagonist's, who told me I'd proven I could string together the twenty-six letters of the alphabet? — *No thanks.* I can't remember her excuse, but it fit the *I-don't-know-how-to-sell-this* mantra.

This went on for several months.

As I carried on wrestling with Twitter and Facebook, blogging and posting flash fiction, I learned about a Stanford Continuing Education course — Using Web 2.0 Tools to Promote Your Fiction. Two novelists taught the class, one of whom had spoken at the mystery conference I attended the previous fall.

The title was intriguing. This might help me with my platform struggles. It might help me figure out Twitter and get me better positioned for that elusive day I landed my agent and the sure-to-follow book deal. And I certainly did not have any clue how to use Web 1.0 tools, whatever those were, much less 2.0, whatever that meant.

The class was held on two successive Saturdays. I walked in hoping to learn how to Tweet more engagingly, and I walked out realizing just how much the internet had changed the world, and how much it was shaking up the publishing industry that I was just starting to get my head around.

Seth Harwood and Scott Sigler gave a brief powerpoint presentation that illustrated how writers were accustomed to going through publishers to reach readers. In the internet age, you could connect directly with readers. Both had built an audience for their work by podcasting their fiction, posting free weekly installments on their websites.

Most of the class involved how to set up a blog — I already knew that — how to podcast, and the tools that were needed.

They're very down-to-earth, funny, personable guys and I was enthused by the idea of using my fiction, rather than a blog and tweets, to reach readers. Because of all the reading I did on how to build a platform, I needed constant reminders that it was my fiction that would connect with readers. Not tweets and Facebook status updates. I guess I'm a slow learner. Very slow.

The rejections from agents continued to litter my inbox and my snail-mailbox. While mulling over the idea of podcasting, I stumbled across Joe Konrath's blog, previously titled — *A Newbie's Guide to Publishing*. I'd read a few of his posts a few years earlier, and the blog crossed my radar again. I don't remember how...Serendipity? After years as a thriller writer with a traditional publisher, Joe was in the throes of exploring self-publishing, blogging about his experiences.

As I read his posts, thought about Seth and Scott's message, and dabbled in podcasting, I started to wonder whether self-publishing might be the way of the future. Was it the right path for me?

During the entire month of June, I battled with the stigma of self-publishing. I talked to my husband about it almost non-stop. At this point, I'd been pursuing a traditionally published career as a writer for nearly ten years. Everything I "knew" about self-publishing was that it was for people who couldn't write very well, people who were too clueless to know what a good story was, who were unteachable and therefore unable to produce good writing. It was for people who printed books and stacked them in their garages. It was for losers and failures and hacks.

Then I thought about Seth and Scott. They were smart, funny guys. I'd read some of their work — they were *good* writers.

And then I thought about people printing their own books with thick glued bindings and blurred, cobbled together covers, the pages inside filled with text that was crooked on the page. I thought about the conventional wisdom that says once an agent and then a publisher accepts your work, you have proven you can write. Before that, you are delusional at best, pathetic at worst.

I read more of Joe's blog. And I began to read the blogs of other writers exploring self-publishing. I slowly began to understand that agent rejection was all about their personal ability to sell a book and quite a lot about what was currently hot in the market. It was about their relationships with editors and personal taste. I thought about the handful of readers I'd attracted with the flash fiction posted on my blog.

I read about how the industry, particularly the Big Six publishers, focused more and more on books they deemed a sure bet instead of offering contracts to writers, knowing it was a multi-year, multi-book investment to grow their readership. I learned that book contracts were getting more and more onerous for writers, locking down not only the rights to a particular novel, but to series characters and the world created in that novel. I read about and saw examples of publishers' poorly conceived book covers and botched or non-existent marketing.

It was the non-existent marketing that really started to shift my thinking.

If I got an agent and a book deal, and then I had to go out and set up my own readings, keep blogging to attract fans, tweet to promote my books, and basically market my books myself, what was the point? Those were the things I needed help with. I wanted to make a living as a writer. With a traditional publisher, I'd receive 8-10% of the list price on a paperback, and I'd have to pay 15% of that to an agent. On an ebook, I'd earn 25%, after the publisher covered their costs. With self-publishing, I could earn 65-70% on ebook sales and a decent percentage on print on demand paperbacks.

In July I made my decision.

The world had changed. Ebooks were growing in popularity, lots of writers were calling themselves indie authors. Some writer who already had successful careers were leaving their publishers, seeking the artistic freedom and financial rewards of going it alone. I bought the domain for Suburban Noir. I integrated my flash fiction blog and my writer blog into one feed so I had a single web presence, per the recommendation of Seth and Scott. I edited my novel AGAIN. There weren't going to be any other eyes on it except my husband's, and it needed to be perfect.

I podcast a few of my unpublished short stories and added those to my online presence. I continued to be a socially awkward tweeter. I kept writing and publishing flash fiction, occasionally submitting to online magazines.

In August, I decided to test the water. I had a cover created and collected eleven of my favorite flash fiction stories. I published it to the ebook stores and didn't tell a soul. I wanted to see what happened.

It sold! Not a lot. But it was flash fiction — extremely short stories, a book that was only seventy pages! And no one knew about it!!

In October I had a setback on the stigma front. I was informed by the editor of Alfred Hitchcock Mystery Magazine that my short story would be in their "Bouchercon" issue. [Bouchercon is the largest mystery-thriller fiction conference in the US.] Because it was being held in San Francisco, I decided on the spur of the moment to attend. (Do I do anything that's not on the spur of the moment?)

At the conference, when I chatted with writers I'd met at the mystery conference a year earlier and mentioned my plan to self-publish, I received chilling looks laced with pity and a sudden end to the conversation. There was one, poorly attended panel on self-publishing. The woman speaking showed paperback copies of her book that exhibited the poor quality my mind associated with self-publishing. I read the first few pages of her book and was dismayed by the poor quality of the writing. I felt like a pariah.

On Saturday night, my husband slept, and I sat near the floor-to-ceiling window on the sixteenth floor for nearly an hour, berating myself for my utter stupidity in choosing to self-publish. I'd tarnished my dreams, spoiled any hope of ever becoming a successful novelist. I'd joined the ranks of those who weren't very good and didn't have the patience and dedication to develop their craft while they sought agent representation. My writing career was over before it started.

In the morning, my husband did his usual job of popping all the self-doubt bubbles, stood me up, dusted me off, and pointed me in the right direction — taking charge of said career.

In November I announced on my blog to my small group of virtual friends, writers all, that I was now an indie author. In the first blog post, I outlined my decision process —

Earlier that year, I'd received an email from a fledgling filmmaker in Melbourne, Australia. He'd read one of my psychological suspense stories on my website and wanted to know if I'd consider allowing him to use it to develop a screenplay. After several months of email, nothing ever came of it, but it illustrated the power of the world wide web to reach readers. I had only a rudimentary website at the time, and someone on the other side of the world found my fiction, liked it, and was able to get in touch with me. I still wasn't entirely clear on what Web 1.0 tools were, but it was definitely a Web 2.0

world and all the old requirements of needing a legacy publisher to print and distribute books while I shouldered the marketing burden were gone.

I blogged about my genre angst. I explored the conventions of noir and described the suburban noir genre as I saw it. I explained that my fiction didn't seem to "fit" in any of the buckets that traditional publishers wanted to look at. (Later, I'd learn I had the same issue with online bookstores, and later still, psychological thrillers that were similar my stories became more popular, so possibly I'd over-thought this, but I over-think everything [a lot of writers do], and I still love the image and suggestion of suburban noir.)

I blogged about the freedom of controlling my cover design and the potential to make a living writing fiction without needing to become a blockbuster bestseller in order to generate a livable income.

The next week I followed up with a blog post about entrepreneurship. I lived in Silicon Valley, the birthplace of high tech start-ups and the dot-com boom and bust and eventual maturity. I explained that going it alone, being an indie author, pursuing my own vision without the blessing of a publisher was in my blood because of where I lived and worked. I breathed it every day, sitting in traffic on Highway 101, eating lunch and going out for drinks in downtown Palo Alto, and reading the local newspaper. Indie was a perfect fit for a writer living in Silicon Valley.

Mostly, I was blogging to myself, trying to shout over the insidious whisper — you're a *self*-published hack.

On December 29, 2010, I published my first novel — *The Demise of the Soccer Moms*.

Within a few days, I was informed by my mother that the book had a typo. I corrected it, reformatted, and re-published to all the ebook stores. Formatting was not so easy in 2010. A day later, a writer acquaintance informed me not too gently that I'd gotten a fact about a movie title wrong (wrong title for the movie I'd referenced). I corrected it, reformatted, and re-published.

Through a cascade of tears, I told my husband we couldn't do this. After the hours and hours of editing and proofing, the reading out loud, not to mention the hours it took to get a book formatted correctly before Scrivener came to save my life, I was exhausted.

A fierce, clawed demon gripped my shoulder and hissed in my ear — *People who self-publish are losers. Their books have mistakes — a self-published novel is a steaming pile of crap. You can call yourself "indie" all you want, compare yourself to an indie musician or filmmaker, an artist with a vision. But you're really just a hack who can't write and therefore can't get an agent, much less a book deal.*

It was a long, long New Year's weekend filled with negative thoughts and utter frustration about how much work this "indie thing" really was. I had no *idea* how much work it really was.

In early January, I picked myself up. I did what other indie writers seemed to be doing. I tweeted. I banded with other indie authors and re-tweeted book links. I asked my online community of writers to read my book. They gave me 4- and 5-star reviews. Some of them asked me to read and review their books. I couldn't always return the 5-star review favor, so I felt slimy. I'm a harsh critic with the fiction I write and the fiction I read. To get an excellent rating, I need to fall in love with a book. I need to be swept off my feet. [I sound strangely and sickeningly like an agent, but I do need to be in love with a novel before I'll rate it five stars.] Those books didn't do that for me, and I felt awful. I was disloyal. I was selfish. I was a snob. I wasn't a supportive writer. Some of those virtual friendships started to deteriorate.

I guest blogged. Other writers guest blogged on my site.

I hosted a blog and Twitter event where I gave away a Kindle.

And I sold books. Quite a few books — over three hundred that first year.

I also got burned out. I was writing another novel. I was writing flash fiction. I was blogging 2-3 days a week. I was reading and commenting on 15-20 writers' blogs in order to return the favor of enhancing blog posts through the comment threads. I was voraciously reading Joe Konrath's posts and the hundreds of comments, eager to learn, straining to think of something to contribute to the conversation that hadn't been said, desperately afraid of being a sycophant like some of the others. Most of all, I was too embarrassed to talk about my one novel and my lackluster sales in the face of romance and thriller and science fiction writers who were selling thousands of books. I was reading and commenting on the KBoards Writer's Cafe.

I was tweeting! I was out of clever, pithy, insightful things to say, if I'd ever said them at all. I agonized over each comment, each tweet, afraid of inviting some of the harsh responses I'd seen thrown at others. I was exhausted. It began to dawn on me that virtual social events were exactly like real life social events — draining for an introvert.

Midway through the year, I began to realize that fiercely promoting a single novel was not going to build a fan base. I received a review that expressed interest in reading more of my books. I didn't have any more books! I had my one little novel. Would they remember me in ten months when my next novel came out? It was doubtful.

As I continued to read agent blogs and other forums the same message was hammered home — you *must* have a platform. Indie authors and marketing gurus concurred — platform! I looked at my tiny platform that was really nothing more than a slick rock in the middle of a rushing river — a few handfuls of writers tweeting and blogging and sharing flash-fiction. My platform consisted of fiction writers. Duh. If I'm a fiction writer, was a blog about the writing life a platform at all? Was it possible, the blasphemous thought came to me, that the agents and marketing gurus were wrong? Could it be, that a blog about writing was not a fiction writer's platform? Could it be, that a fiction writer's platform is *fiction*? Maybe what I needed to do was write more fiction.

For several years before I published my novel, I'd had an idea knocking around my head for a mystery series featuring a quirky administrative assistant at a suburban church. This outwardly mildly ditzy, but inwardly intelligent young woman would solve crimes through illogically drawn conclusions from the Bible and The National Enquirer. Maybe now was the time to launch this. All the experts said series were a good way to build a fan base. Readers got hooked on a character and came back for more.

At one point I'd written a short story based on the character. I pulled it out and started doing some research. The first thing I noticed was that The National Enquirer no longer published the stories I remembered from the headlines flashing in my face from supermarket racks when I was a child. *Woman Has Alien Baby! Dog and Cat Give Birth to a Dat!!* The supermarket tabloids were celebrity-focused. I wasn't sure my idea would work for that reason, and for the sheer absurdity of it.

But I liked the character. The only trouble was, I didn't want to write a full-blown mystery. I still wanted to write psychological suspense. I decided to write a novella series. It would have a lighter mystery. I still liked the idea of a church secretary because the church setting would provide an endless stream of conflict.

I started writing in first person, a voice I'd never tried before. My fingers flew across the keys. I was having fun. Then, about forty percent of the way into the novella, a ghost appeared. Oh shit! How did that happen? I'd never written a ghost story. I'd only read a few in my lifetime. What was I going to do with a ghost? I went around in circles and finally decided to follow where the story was leading. So a novella, suburban noir, Madison Keith, ghost story, mystery series was born. Talk about a genre mashup. But I had fun writing it. I published it and decided I'd write three a year.

By the end of 2011, I'd published two novels, three novellas, and a second collection of flash fiction. Throughout that year, there were endless ups and downs. Formatting was a nightmare, and my husband and I had many tense moments trying to get a process in place. Some of the tools were geared for PCs, and I am a Mac zealot. Sales were intermittent. I ran some ads in ebook newsletters, books sold, and then sales petered out. Then I'd have another spurt of three or four sales.

I tried to calm myself. My husband, the patron saint of patience, kept me focused on writing. Or he tried. I wrote, but I worried. I cried. I poured over Joe's blog trying to figure out the secret to the success of the writers posting there. I questioned. I felt the burn of the stigma branded onto my forehead — *self-published*.

But something kept me going.

I'm A Writer

At some point, I can't say when, I started calling myself a writer. I said it softly. Hesitantly. I put competitive analyst/writer on my tax return! I wrote it on a customs form, once. The change came after self-publishing my second or third novel. That's strange to me, because as a person who focused on traditional publishing for so long, I would have thought publishing a handful of short stories, or earlier, when I was writing a weekly column for my local newspaper, I might have evolved to the mindset of calling myself a writer. I didn't.

Possibly, it's my husband who should get the credit. When I whined on a bi-weekly basis — *I want to be a writer* (meaning not working at this boring-as-shit job as a competitive analyst), he repeated back like I'd volleyed a ping-pong ball at him — *You are a writer*. Maybe he said that so many times, so consistently, never varying the words, always the same steady tone of voice, that it finally seeped into my brain. When I split hairs about *earning a living as a writer*, he repeated — *You are a writer*.

Eventually, the self-publishing venture became smoother. Sort of. I discovered Scrivener — a writing tool which produces clean, elegant, well-formatted e-pub files. Lightning Source, my print-on-demand vendor, began offering matte book covers, which made me feel my print books looked more like trade paperbacks instead of oversized mass market paperbacks with their shiny, less elegant covers.

By early 2015, I'd published six novels, eleven novellas, a few short stories, and five collections of flash fiction. In the fall of 2015, the ghost story novella series was complete.

In the midst of writing the third novella in the series, a huge part of her backstory opened up and began an ongoing thread that was resolved in the eleventh novella. It brought the series to a natural conclusion. I felt satisfied and also ready to move on. The series found a few fans who were disappointed to see it end, but I was ready for something new. At the same time, I couldn't let go of the ghosts. An abandoned ship docked at a pier near my new home inspired me to write a trilogy that imagined a ghost haunting the bowels of the ship.

Sales continued to be hit and miss. I was able to get my trilogy and a few other novels into a local bookstore where I sold a handful a month. I did some paperback giveaways on GoodReads and ebook giveaways on Amazon which resulted in a few new fans. Over half of my books had no reviews. There's a marketing reason for that, and I'll write about reviews later in this book. I was very, very discouraged.

Constantly looking for inspiration from others' experiences, I was enthused a few years earlier when I read a comment by a writer who said she didn't see a steady uptick in sales until she'd published three novels. When I passed that milestone, discouragement returned. Then I read about writers seeing traction after five novels. That milestone had also come and gone. Discouragement was my constant companion, and I battled to get it out of my writing room nearly every day.

If a tree falls in the forest and no one hears…if a writer publishes books and no one reads…is she truly a writer?

I read an article stating that despite the ebook revolution creating space for stories to find their natural length, despite the fact that readers were pressed for time and thus drawn to shorter fiction, novels still sell much better than short stories or novellas. Clearly, I'd focused on the wrong form, even though that's what the story called for and I'd loved writing all my shorter pieces. Hoping to draw readers craving longer books, I bundled my novellas into novel-length collections. They continued to languish on the shelves. I changed the cover of the first book in the series, hoping for the magical burst in sales that many people claimed resulted from a cover change. Not for me.

Across all of the ebook stores, I was seeing about 10-20 downloads a week of my free flash fiction and the first novella in the Madison Keith series (also free). Excerpts from my novels were in the backs of the flash fiction collections. I considered this a good move, something that would attract readers, but it wasn't to be. Despite the gurus who claim samples in the back of every book are a must, they didn't work for me, even in novels. Who knows why. Who knows why anything works or doesn't in the publishing world.

Since the venture started, I'd sold over a thousand books. That was no small feat. But I wanted to make a living. Despite the odds against that, despite the conventional wisdom that only a handful of writers found that kind of success, I wouldn't let go. The high odds were in the past. In self-publishing, it was absolutely possible. Writers were proving it every day.

It's what I'd dreamed of nearly all my life, and I wasn't giving up, no matter how many marketing tactics failed for me. There had to be a way. Then, I began seeing blog posts that writers found their audiences with their seventh book, their tenth book. Hope resurrected! But most of those were series. Once again, I was on the outskirts with standalone novels and a novella series that couldn't figure out its genre.

It looked like 2015 was going to be a busy year. I had three novels in the pipeline, two novellas, and had resurrected this book — part memoir, part informative, and, I hoped, part inspiration. Within months, I'd abandoned it again.

I took a workshop on becoming more productive, and it helped a lot in clueing me in with greater clarity to the voice of the internal critic — the voice of fear — and recognizing its insidious presence inside my writing room. The workshop freed me and enabled me to actually *write* when I shut the door to my writing room instead of perusing blogs for the "secret" to finding an audience for my fiction, for inspiration to keep going.

Traditional publishing was becoming more and more unfavorable to writers, and I knew I'd made the right choice. I knew I'd be facing the same obstacles if I'd taken that path. *If* I'd found an agent and a publisher. Taking that route, my books would be gone from bookstore shelves within a few months of publication, if they even made it in to begin with. The stigma in the public and my own head receded. I rarely felt it. I truly felt like an entrepreneur, an indie author. The shared data from indie authors over the past few years has proven I made the choice that offers the greatest potential for making a living at writing fiction.

I still wasn't even close to making that living. But I knew I'd never give up — I'm a writer until the day I die.

Overnight Success...Or Not

For decades I've been writing and submitting, publishing, and then self-publishing fiction. A few years ago, I wrote down for the first time that my dream was to be on the New York Times bestseller list. I shared those words with a handful of others, feeling like an utter fool, knowing how the NYT list is selectively compiled, pulling their data from a curated selection of bookstores.

I hadn't even realized I wanted that, but when I was urged to put my dreams in writing, it was the first thing that appeared on my laptop screen, uncensored. I wonder if having the guts to put that in writing for someone else to mock broke something loose in the universe. A few months later, I was contacted by my first-ever rabid fan, the kind of fan I long for. The kind of fan who I worried was only in my dreams. Her messages were followed by another long dry spell. Then Kirkus Reviews, where I'd submitted a novel for a professional review, told me my book review was in the top 10% of indie reviews and asked whether I wanted to promote it. Still far too eager for external validation, I thought this meant "something". I'm blushing as I write this. I spent my annual bonus from my day job to promote the review and the book through Kirkus.

Crickets.

On a rainy Autumn evening, my sister was having a glass of wine at a bar in Carmel, California. She met an editor from

HarperCollins Witness Impulse. My sister told the editor I was a writer and the editor's ears *perked up* at the idea of Suburban Noir. At the editor's invitation, I contacted her. She wrote back that from what she could tell on my website, my books would be an *excellent addition* to the HC Witness Impulse line. She was particularly interested in two of my novels and asked for the complete manuscripts. I sent them. (Yes, I was wavering in my decision. Big time.)

That same month, I received a message through my website from a freelance producer with a "deal at ABC studios" wanting to know if film/TV rights were available for the book I'd promoted through Kirkus.

I never heard back from the HarperCollins editor. I never heard back from the producer. My fan had read all my books. I continued writing, and sales trickled along — a handful a day, sometimes less.

I cherished every single sale, but the idea of supporting our family of two with my fiction was still a vaporous dream.

MOTIVE

FINDING YOUR VOICE

Who Are You?

"The thing that is really hard and really amazing is giving up on being perfect and beginning the work of becoming yourself." — Anna Quindlen

"They [agents] didn't want my book, I believe, because there was nothing else like it out there at the time. They had no recent precedent. They couldn't wrap it up in a genre and market it." — Unknown

It's very likely that my fiction is not the misfit I think it is. The genre is crime fiction or psychological thriller, according to most bookstores, but not really. Does it conform to those conventions? No. When law enforcement representatives appear in my novels, they're minor characters. The story isn't about solving a crime which is the key feature of most crime fiction and most psychological thrillers. In my stories, the thrills take place over a kitchen sink as two characters face battles to the death inside their minds rather than on the precipice of an icy canyon.

Hundreds of thousands of books, possibly millions, do not fit neatly into a specified genre, neatly ticking all the boxes for what readers expect, and more importantly, crave in that kind of story.

Thinking about genre is both a help and a trap.

Of course there are different types of stories people like to read, and they look for signals that a novel will provide the familiar characters and themes they find satisfying. When I see a book that has a crime, but there's no mention of a detective or someone from law enforcement as the protagonist, I'm likely to give it a deeper look. When I read one-star reviews complaining that the characters are "unlikable", I'm much more likely to love the story.

I like to read crime and literary fiction, which generally

delivers darker stories and more complicated, contradictory characters, because I read fiction to make sense of the world. Yes, I want to escape from the details of my life, but not to live in a futuristic or dystopian world, not to see the planet saved by a hero that roots out pervasive conspiracies, and not to feel the thrill of falling in love. Yes, there's an element of fantasy in all fiction — living inside another person's head and experiencing lives that are different from mine. But mostly I want to sort things out, I want to think, I want to understand other people better, I want to return to my life with a fresh perspective. For me, stories about typical people who are driven by circumstances to commit crimes they never imagined helps me understand human beings pushed to the extreme edges of life.

Writers are advised to write what they like to read, and I can't comprehend how you could do anything else. Still, a lot of advice to indie writers suggests writing what sells or what's currently popular. It's not suggested that writers choose a genre they loathe, but they are told with a great deal of authority to find a popular genre that's aligned with what they like to read. It's a fine line, but also a large gap.

I can't imagine a lot of satisfaction in writing in a genre for the sole purpose of selling books. I tried that, and I didn't even make it to seeing the book accepted for publication because I walked away. I can't imagine establishing a unique voice by writing to conform to the market because a large part of a writer's voice grows out of the things that move her, the things that he's obsessed with. If a writer is only writing a certain type of fiction because it has a large audience, those things that stir emotions and reveal obsessions aren't going to be as powerful because they'll be shaped to fit the genre conventions.

It all comes down to this elusive thing called Voice. There are entire books on the subject of voice. There are exercises for finding and developing one's voice. And then character voice is thrown into the mix. It's all a little confusing and sometimes feels like nothing but vapor.

After twisting myself into knots on this topic, working through those voice exercises and discovering only more vapor, I finally realized my voice is me. It's what I think about, what I'm passionate about, what I worry about, and what I fear. It's what horrifies me and makes me laugh and makes me cry. It's the things that fill me with rage.

My voice is the convoluted way I put sentences together and often interrupt myself. My voice is my neuroses and my suburban upbringing. It's the status and shape the world was in when I came of age, and the neighborhood I grew up in. My voice comes from the public schools I attended and the college where I half-heartedly studied history. It's my taller-than-average height and my German-Czechoslovakian-Italian blood. It's my early childhood in New York state and my growing up in San Jose, California. It's my nightmares and my losses and failures and successes.

I'm a suburban white girl. I'm desperately worried about the care and preservation of our planet. I like wine and martinis and scotch. I hate soda pop. I love to eat, and I love walking on the beach. My voice grew out of the years I spent working in high tech, feeling like a fish out of water at all times. I'm conflicted about the issue of homelessness, and I adore animals and am terrified of large spiders. I can go on and on.

What do I do with all of that?

When I write fast, my voice emerges. I'm not filtering who I am. I'm letting the raw stuff inside my head transform into characters and stories.

First, my voice consists of the kinds of characters I invent and the problems I toss into their lives like hand grenades. It's the settings that appeal to me. After that, it's some ephemeral thing inside of me, that when I type as fast as I can, emerges onto the screen. It's me and my imagination, unfiltered. And the faster I can write, the faster my fingertips stomp on the fears that keep my voice from making itself heard.

As the Cheshire Cat asks Alice In Wonderland — *Who **are** you?*

Boring!

Maybe this is boring.

Has that thought ever crossed your mind while you're editing or revising your work? Worse, has it floated like a heavy, dark cloud over the flow of a story coming from your mind to your fingertips, settling down until your hands froze and your brain rushed off to Twitter or Facebook or a snack to escape the crushing discovery that your writing is *BORING*?

Maybe *I'm* boring.

First, this idea assumes the experience of boredom is universal. I find football boring. Half of America finds thrills in football games every single weekend. Often people look at me as if I've lost my mind when I say I love sitting in a five-foot by twelve-foot room for hours every single day of the week. I can see they want to scratch out their eyes at the thought of something so boring.

A man I knew for over ten years when I was working in high tech bored me to tears. When I saw his name on my caller-ID, I felt a hard lump in my stomach. When I saw him walking down the hall, I turned the corner, if possible. Others in my group listened to him for hours, posing questions, drawing him out, fascinated by his technical knowledge.

I like classical piano music and literary fiction and sitting on the beach, staring at the ocean. I love playing golf, and I'm on the edge of my seat when I watch televised golf tournaments.

Millions of people find those pastimes mind-numbingly boring.

Fear of being boring is a fear of being yourself. Fear that you aren't good enough, that something is lacking. It's fear that you have to be someone else to be a good writer. This doesn't mean there are elements of craft that are used to develop strong pacing and heighten tension.

Kristine Kathryn Rusch, who writes a business blog for writers, said that often a writer believes her work is boring because the voice is familiar. That familiar voice is talking to you twenty-four-seven.

During the editing process, take a step back and consider whether a line or a paragraph or a chapter is "boring" because it needs some revision, or if you're rejecting the echo of your voice. It's a delicate, often hair-thin line, but know that line is there. Don't slice the soul out of your story when that gnawing voice whispers — *This is boring*. Get a second opinion

As the words flow out of your head, through your hands, onto the keyboard in a first draft, keep writing no matter how loudly that voice shrieks and wails. Decide later.

Literary Envy

"Prose is architecture, not interior design..." — Ernest Hemingway

"Our words are in service to our story, not the other way around."

I don't know the source of that second line, whether it belongs to Hemingway or someone commenting on his comment. Either way, I wish I'd read that years ago.

It's lost in the dust of my memory why and when I started thinking I wanted to write literary fiction. Possibly because the books about becoming a writer that I was drawn to early on had that bent, or possibly because of the handful of writing classes I took. Possibly because that's primarily what I was reading at the time. I expect it was a combination of all three, alongside the cachet of the New York Times Book Review and books that tended to be promoted in the media.

I wanted to write literature. I wanted to write meaningful stories (whatever that meant) and craft seductive sentences. I devoured John Updike and Phillip Roth and Tom Perrotta, Ian McEwan and Joyce Carol Oates. Yet when I wrote, my voice, more of a whisper at the time, sounded very different. I was the product of suburban public schools. I wasn't steeped in classics and history and philosophy. My literary education was light. My international travel history when I graduated from college consisted of a single visit to Canada and a teenaged day trip to Tijuana where I could drink alcohol before I was twenty-one. Within the United States, I'd been on family vacations to visit relatives on the east coast, and lots of camping in California state parks. Not the stuff of broadening one's cultural and political literary muscles.

I know now that those literary voices came from a place I've never been, from a life I never lived.

I read Richard Russo and the short stories in the New Yorker. Oh, how I wanted to write like that. Like all of them.

My stories sounded flat beside those! My subjects were nothing like theirs. I have notebooks and computer files full of aborted attempts to be "literary".

It terrified me that there was a women's fiction-y sound to my writing. As a fairly solid feminist, I despise the term women's fiction. There's fiction. There's non-fiction. Men write stories of family and marriage and career, and they're deemed novelists. Women write the same, and they're relegated to the ladies' section. But I digress.

When I discovered Ruth Rendell and Patricia Highsmith, I began to see there was a shadowy, vaguely defined "thing" called literary crime. I wondered whether that might be within my reach. I found Tana French and Gillian Flynn. I looked at the novels and stories of Ian McEwan and Joyce Carol Oates with new eyes and realized how often crime was a theme in their work. I still knew I'd never write like them, heck, I'll never write as well as Ms. Rendell either. I won't get started on the soul-satisfying language of nearly every book I've read that comes from an author who was born and raised in the UK.

But I can't change my voice. I can't be someone else, someone I'm not, putting on the mask and costume of a stranger with different life experiences and education and all the other factors that make up a human being. I can only be me.

When my moody short story about the aftermath of a crime received an honorable mention from Joyce Carol Oates in the Zoetrope All-Story Short Fiction contest, I cried. The next morning I woke pinching myself. I could hardly breathe for weeks. I'm not one of those great writers I love and admire, and I'll never write as well as they do, but maybe my writing has a slight literary quality. Whether or not that's true, I can't change that either. My voice is my voice. I can't try to be literary any more than I can try to be funny or smart or witty. Trying will produce writing that's false and dull, voiceless.

This chapter is called literary envy, but maybe that's not the right term. It's about loving great writers and great books. Even writers that others don't love and don't consider all that great. It's loving their voices, and then closing the door and letting my voice speak its mind. It's always striving to improve. It's reading great writing and letting that sink into my bone marrow.

In an exercise addressing my thoughts about fear and self-criticism, I wrote this:

I like finely crafted sentences that satisfy me when I'm reading. I like interesting language and the sound of words and sentences and paragraphs. That doesn't mean I like fiction that's just those things, overwrought and flowery, lacking a compelling story. I don't want words over characters. I want to be lost in the experience, but for me, the language is part of that experience. The writers I love draw me into a story and make me forget I'm reading while still touching a poetic note with their style, satisfying me on multiple levels.

As I'm writing this, I'm questioning whether it's really "language" and sentences I'm enjoying when I read. Maybe it's the way they dig so deep? Or their themes? I'm really not sure.

I suspect I have conflicting goals – wanting to make a living writing fiction, and wanting to write fiction that's as "literary" or as "good" as I'm capable of [do not ask me to define literary…it's an I-know-it-when-I-see-it thing].

What is "good" writing? There is some objectivity in that assessment, but it's also highly subjective, aka taste. So maybe when I say I want to be a "good" writer, I don't even know what that means! Maybe it means fiction that suits my taste, and isn't necessarily objectively "good" at all.

Ms. Oates has been severely criticized for her writing style, a style I adore. So maybe when I say I want to be a good writer, what I really want is to read my own fiction and get the pleasure I get from writers I love, which is probably not even possible! It's only possible in the writing itself, not in the re-reading.

Maybe I want to find that audience that will love my fiction as much as I love my favorite writers. And maybe that is all about **voice** and not about some external standard of "good" writing. I want to write fiction that readers can't put down, that offers intriguing characters and surprises in the plot, and delivers satisfying endings. And melodic language.

In *Fearless Writing*, William Kenower says — "To get into the flow, put aside the notion of 'good' and 'bad'. Think only of this — have I said what I wanted to say?"

This is my new compass.

More About "Bad" Writing

"**B**ad writing precedes good writing. This is an infallible rule, so don't waste time trying to avoid bad writing. (That just slows down the process.) Anything committed to 'paper' can be changed. The idea is to start, and then go from there." — Unknown

This has been said in many different ways by hundreds, if not thousands of writers. The essence of simply getting started is captured in the pervasive belief in the "shitty first draft", an idea attributed to Hemingway that "all first drafts are shit".

"Bad" writing is also the ominous, authoritative voice of the established publishing industry flinging mud at self-published writers.

Of course, there are rules of grammar and sentence structure. There are techniques in character development and plotting and pacing and dialog and story arc that if they aren't mastered lead to unappealing writing. But in many ways, "bad" writing is writing that doesn't fit one's personal tastes.

Millions of readers loved the infamous erotica trilogy that began with *Fifty Shades of Grey*. Bad writing didn't enter most readers' reaction to the books. Readers devoured the trilogy, and sales exploded as it was recommended by word of mouth and then read out of curiosity to find out what all the fuss was about. Others were shocked at the downfall of literature illustrated in those pages, completely unable to comprehend why a story with cliché́d phrases and easy-to-read sentences and a barely-there plot and stock characters was so popular. The sounds of mockery grew to a cacophony. But millions loved the stories.

When self-publishing began to surge thanks to the growing popularity of Kindle Desktop Publishing (KDP) and other platforms, the literary community warned relentlessly of the coming "tsunami of crap". The same community that was appalled by *Fifty Shades*, published by the venerable Random House, worried about the quality of self-published books while raking in money from a book with writing and story-telling that was weaker than thousands of independently published novels.

Self-publishing was bringing this "tsunami of crap" because the writers who were uploading their manuscripts to KDP hadn't graduated from writing programs. They hadn't been edited by the "right pros" and vetted by agents. They hadn't "paid their dues" trying to jump the gates before they were "ready".

In traditional publishing, it's a badge of courage to have a file folder full of rejection letters. I treasured mine for years. The theory is that if one keeps writing and submitting her work, the very act of re-writing to try to win acceptance, writing successive stories and novels, improves a writer's skills and when she's "ready" her work will be accepted and published, after more re-writes and thorough professional editing, of course.

Learning the craft absolutely matters, but does learning it while being rejected by a single editor's choice rather than making it available to readers with an enormous range of tastes make the writing better?

Taste masquerades as judgments of "good" and "bad" writing. Choose any writer of note, and there will be vicious critics of her work. All books that sell widely have reader reviews that stomp on the "writing". Cries for better editorial oversight fill the one- and two-star reviews.

Among themselves, writers laugh at agent feedback where one declares the writing is weak and another praises its genius.

Often it's not even clear what "bad writing" refers to. Is it the flaws of *Fifty Shades*? Is it flaunting the rules of grammar? Is it simply the sin of being dry or dull? Is it a certain type of story?

If a reader notices the writing, feeling it pull them out of the story, that reader experiences "bad writing'. Some readers want minimalist language in the stories they read. Others love to immerse themselves in artfully constructed sentences and word use, as if the reader is sinking into a steaming bath filled with fragrant bubbles.

I worry constantly about bad writing. My writing has been praised and eviscerated.

One reviewer stated — *You can't just string a bunch of words together and call it a novel*. Or something to that effect. Fortunately, I haven't memorized the harsh review, as I was prone to do when I first received negative reviews. Right below her comment, another reader gushes that *the writing is excellent* and she *lost herself* in the story.

Have I become a "better" writer over the years? I have no objective way to measure that. I hope so. I believe so. It seems that's how it should work. But I also wonder if I've simply developed confidence. The structure of a plot feels more infused into my DNA now. I've stopped censoring my first drafts because I truly believe better writing comes out of uncensored writing, followed by revisions and rigorous editing.

So if you're worried you're not a "good" writer, or "good enough", just keep writing. It sounds absurdly simplistic and also defiant, but it's true. Your words are good enough for readers you connect with, and whether you judge a book's success by sales or by praise from those who read voraciously, opinions will always vary, as opinions do.

When you find your readers, they will call you brilliant — a genius. Those who don't connect with your voice will use other adjectives.

In the end, the key question is — "Have I said what I wanted to say?"

Unlikable Characters Take Two

Readers and book reviewers have informed me, repeatedly, with outrage, that my characters are not likable.

Those giving advice on finding success as a writer are firm on this point — you must have a protagonist readers can root for. My writing teacher badgered me about this. Agents opine about it. Peers helping their writer friends preach the mantra of heroines and heroes. There's an entire framework for writing fiction called the hero's journey.

The unlikable character issue created years of self-doubt in my writing. Periodically I asked myself, should I make them nicer? Should I give them puppies as my writing teacher suggested? I think what she was trying to say, in an awkward way, was give them something that makes them more well-rounded. Something accessible. It doesn't have to be a damn puppy. It can be a feral cat they're compelled to feed.

Then I read *The Irresistible Novel: How to Craft an Extraordinary Story That Engages Readers from Start to Finish*. A long title with a lot to say inside.

The author talks about a psychological term — "theory of mind". He says we surmise that while someone else has another mind, we think we can still understand it. At the root of our need, our craving for story is the idea that, *If it happened to him, it could happen to me, so I'd better take note*. The author, Jeff Gerke, goes on to say:

"Story works only if we believe it could be us out there, hunted by those sharp-toothed devils. **If the person in the story seems very unlike who we think we are** [emphasis added] — maybe goofy Uncle Rogg, who likes to strap himself with bacon and spend the night on the ground far from everyone else — then we won't take the lesson to heart. We won't even really care about the story. Serves him right for being stupid. But make the hero of the story seem like the person reading the story, and suddenly we're all ears."

Just when I thought I'd accepted my voice and the characters that drew me to them with their hurting, angry, jealous, paranoid voices, I was right back where I'd started. I felt I was being told I needed Heroines with an upper case H. But Heroines don't interest me. They're superhuman. In fact, they seem very *un*like the flawed person I've known inside of me all my life.

Finally, after years on this vicious circle of the stories I was drawn to versus the stories that were deemed salable, it dawned on me — readers who are aware of and in touch with their dark side will see themselves in my characters. Readers who aren't as aware of their flaws, will not. End of story.

I saw this in the reviews of Gone Girl. Many people hated the protagonist, a bright, vengeful sociopath.

But do you know what? I saw myself in her. I saw the awareness of what it means to be the cool girl and how you feel you have to be that girl for guys to like you. I felt that in my job, even if it wasn't about searching for a mate, it was about being part of the boys' club in a male-dominated industry. Even more important, the driving force of Amy Dunn's life was that she wanted and needed her husband to love her so deeply he remembered every detail of every moment they spent together.

I saw myself in that! The desire to be loved so deeply that you consume another person's thoughts. And in that little sliver of likeness, I followed her in horror as I saw where such feelings, if uncontrolled, can lead. And I saw myself in Nick — his refusal to be consumed, his desire to pull away into himself and not allow someone to possess his soul. It was very much a cautionary tale.

Gillian Flynn, the author of *Gone Girl*, and the creative genius behind Amy and Nick Dunn once said that likability is never a reason she reads novels. She doesn't read for a "hero narrative". She felt no need to root for someone to overcome. What interests her is "why people do what they do, good and bad". This is what interests me. It's a question I've been chastised for asking too often throughout my life — *Why?*

As a child, playacting with her friends, Gillian Flynn said she wanted to be the witch, not the princess. In her view, the witch had the interesting story, the princess was simply good, and women aren't inherently good. She likes very complicated, dark characters.

After years of doubting the characters that came to me, I've slowly learned to give them free rein — I'm madly in love with my unlovable characters, just as a number of people manage to love sometimes unlovable me.

DARK DAYS

Fighting Discouragement

Repeatedly over the years, I checked book sales with the delusional idea that seeing additional sales would encourage me that success was coming, however slowly.

No. This doesn't work. For me, it was encouraging at times, devastating more often than not.

Nineteen days into the month of April 2015, after four years of self-publishing, discouraged over my lack of readers, frustrated with my work-in-progress, I checked sales in the afternoon. Two books sold. *Two*. Both sales were copies of books in my 99-cent Cocktail Fiction collection, one of which was bought by a good friend. I knew that sale was to a friend because she told me. And because that same friend also mentioned she'd read my second novel, I realized the single sale of that book, which I'd celebrated wildly the month before was also to her! So all I'd really sold to new readers the previous month were two copies of my first novel. I was grateful for those two new readers. Grateful, but...

I was beyond depressed.

And this wasn't the first time. I was the ultimate cliché — the *self-published hack* who sold books to her mother, a few friends, and a handful of strangers. Okay, several hundred, but it felt like handfuls. And those friends who did read my books were a count-on-one-hand group among the family friends who mostly ignored my writing entirely.

Maybe "just writing" and expanding my bookshelf, the strategy I'd been pursuing for three years, wasn't a strategy at all. *Build it, and they will come.* Only if they can find you. Maybe I really did need to market my fiction, not that I had a clue how to do that.

The next day, I managed to extract myself from the pit of despair. I reminded myself that one sale a month was worth celebrating. I reminded myself to celebrate *every single* reader

who spent a dollar of her hard-earned money to read one of my
books.

    Every. Single. Dollar.

    Every. Single. Reader.

The Green-Eyed Monster

When I was ten, my eight-year-old sister got a new camera for her birthday. It was the latest model — a sleek new Kodak Instamatic. My camera was a clunky, boxy plastic thing called a Brownie, I think. I don't know what I said, or what I did, but after my sister had finished opening her gifts, my mother pulled me into another room and said, "Your green eyes are showing, and it's not very attractive."

It wasn't fair! I was older. I should have had the newest, coolest thing. My camera was designed for a child. Hers was cool — silver and black, slim and sleek to my gray plastic box. She had a camera made for a teenager, and she was eight!

As John Lennon said, "I'm just a jealous guy."

I want what I want. It's not that I don't want someone else to have it. I didn't want to take my sister's camera, I didn't want her to have mine while I had hers, I just wanted the cool one, and I wanted it first. I *deserved* it because I was older.

I wanted people to *discover*, then read and enjoy my books and stories. But I wanted more than that. I wanted to support myself full time as a writer. I longed to walk away from my day job and live the remainder of my working years in a career that satisfied me and thrilled me and drew me out of bed every morning with eager anticipation. I love writing fiction so much that I don't care if I work beyond the expected age of retirement. I could write fiction until I'm blind, and beyond. I could write fiction until my hands curl into petrified claws.

I was jealous of people who got there ahead of me. Jealous of traditionally published writers who managed to find that magic streak and over the years, turned it into a living. Jealous of blockbuster writers who worked hard and then saw their book sales skyrocket them to the top of a bestseller list, New York Times or others. I was jealous of indie authors who managed to make it all click in the space of two or three years. Granted, they'd been writing before they found life-changing success, but so had I.

Watching indie writers who started self-publishing the same year I did turn out more books, and climb onto the rungs of bestseller lists, and worst of all, seeing lists of writers who quit their jobs hollowed me out with jealousy. Reading blogs about the thrill of walking away from the corporate world to follow the love of your life made me crazy with envy.

I wanted that.

I wanted that so badly I got up six days a week at four o'clock in the morning. I wanted that so badly I avoided eating lunch with my co-workers so I could race through my workday and eke out another twenty or thirty minutes on my novel. I wanted that so badly that on weekends, sun shining, others out socializing, I sat cross-legged, tapping my keyboard, re-reading my words, cutting and re-writing, editing, and polishing until they came the closest I could get to communicating the story in my head.

Of course I didn't think I *deserved* it, like I thought I deserved that camera. The adult me knows that no one deserves anything. But maybe a small part of me does think I deserve it. I've worked at this for years. Yes, sometimes I see all my failures — all the times I could have been writing and didn't, all the opportunities I had to get my work out there and held back. But beneath it all, the child inside was screaming — "I worked just as hard as they did to develop my craft. I worked harder than he did. I worked for more years and more hours than she did. I *deserve* it too."

Jealousy is a difficult feeling to describe. It's painful and sickening. It makes me feel small. Sometimes it makes me angry. No one really knows why one writer discovers a fanatical and significant audience before another. Everyone has theories — superior story-telling skills, the right book at the right time, well-written books, lots of books, a lucky break, spot-on marketing, instinctive social media skills. Some of those things are required, all are helpful, but many writers have all of that and still spend their days in a cubicle, late nights or pre-dawn hours on a laptop.

The easiest, and best way to keep it from gnawing at my soul was to keep working. The easiest way to fling open the door and allow it to creep inside my mind and devour me was to spend too much time on the internet. Even helpful forums and blogs that encouraged indie authors and shared ideas had the potential to backfire as success stories are casually shared and held up as examples —

I put out my third novel, and my books just took off.

I don't advertise, I just chat on Facebook.

I have ten thousand newsletter subscribers, and they all buy my new novel the first day it's out.

Comparing oneself with others is never productive, but when the writing world is filled with successful writers who truly want to help others get where they are, the natural result is advice. And advice, as I said, can blow up in your face —

I did all those same things, followed all the suggestions, and I'm still not finding a solid audience.

My organic reviews are hit and miss. I go months without a new one.

My newsletter has two hundred subscribers, and I only get a handful more each month.

I'm a dweeb on social media.

About half the time, I've always known my day will come. About half the time, a rat sits inside of me, sharp teeth chewing on my heart, wanting what someone else has, what so many others have. Wanting thousands of devoted fans waiting for my next book, wanting a day where I sleep in until five!

A life where I didn't have to schedule phone calls with family and friends because I was trying to juggle two full-time jobs. A life where I wasn't looking out the window during a meeting in which my co-workers discussed the intricate details of technology and revenue growth, sucking my soul dry.

All I could do was keep on keeping on, writing and not comparing the number of books I'd published and my sales rank and my voice and my genre and my pricing and my reviews and my very soul to people I didn't even know.

INTO THE LIGHT

Everything Is Writeable About

"And by the way, everything in life is writeable about if you have the outgoing guts to do it, and the imagination to improvise. The worst enemy to creativity is self-doubt."
—Sylvia Plath

When you're running your own business, which you are doing when you step onto the path of the indie author, you are in charge. This is thrilling, terrifying, and a recipe for self-doubt. After twenty years in the corporate world, following nearly two decades in rather dictatorial religious traditions and the authoritarian, conformist structure of public education, I was used to doing what I was told. In those worlds, opportunities, where you're invited to think for yourself, are infrequent.

The choices and creative control open to an indie author are seemingly endless.

First, and most important, I have complete creative control over what I write. If a story that strikes me is too short for a novel, too long for a short story, I can write and publish a novella. I can write the characters who speak to me and the plot lines that intrigue me. I can continue a series as long as I'd like or end it when I choose, with only the readers to answer to. I don't have a publishing company focused on their profit margin line telling me what the life of my series will be. Only my own profit margin needs to enter my thoughts.

When I want to extend the space between series releases and write a standalone novel, I can do that. No marketing department tells me it isn't in the plan. I can release books as I write them instead of waiting nine to eighteen months while my work is slotted into a schedule of corporate choosing.

I can write psychological suspense and suburban noir and psychological thrillers and ghost stories. Instead of my eclectic work confusing the brand that's been defined by a publisher, I can build my brand for those genres around my name.

I choose the images and design of my covers. I decide how sales-y my blurbs are, and how heavy the editorial hand will be. I decide when, where, and how I'll advertise and promote my books.

The choices are endless, and it's all on me and my partner. So the opportunity to question my choices comes weekly, and sometimes, daily.

Maybe the cover is inhibiting sales. Do I change it? Do readers really shun books because the cover isn't exactly like the others in that genre? Or maybe, since my books don't fit neatly into a genre, an unusual cover is a good thing — advertising that this is something slightly different.

I've re-written blurbs dozens of times, wondering if I'm hitting the right note, faithfully representing my books, attracting readers who will enjoy the story. I've tried numerous social media strategies which are detailed elsewhere in this book. I've questioned my release schedule for my books, my mixed genres, writing to market, and how much time to invest in local bookstore promotion. I've read different theories on pricing and changed my book prices more times than I can count.

In all of these areas, results are not immediate, and most of the time, not clear-cut enough to measure. So I'm left with self doubt and second-guessing.

At the end of the day, the only solution is to go with what feels right at the time. It's that, or lose my mind in endless conversations with my husband, circular discussions in which I change my mind mid-sentence. Being in charge is scary, and sometimes overwhelming, but mostly, it's wonderful.

And finally, back to the Sylvia Plath quote that opened this chapter.

My writing has taken me down some unexpected paths. I expected to write a light, quirky mystery series about an amateur sleuth, not a collection of books filled with ghosts — some terrifying, some mild. I never in a thousand years expected to write about a sociopath who becomes a vigilante killer. The stories that emerged had religious and feminist themes. I didn't expect that, but I followed my creative voice.

Many times, I doubted what I was writing. Not *as* I was writing. During those times, the thrill of the story unfolding at my fingertips is too exciting. But re-reading what I'd written? Revising what I'd written? Making choices about what stays and goes? Deciding to stick with the stories that came out of my subconscious mind? All of that stirred up self-doubt.

In the end, mustering up my *outgoing guts*, I found that everything truly is *writable* about.

What Joe Knows

One of my favorite blog posts from Joe Konrath is titled, *Here's What I Know*, posted in March of 2014, and just as relevant several years later. He's provided books of information on his blog regarding his self-publishing experience.

Since that post in 2014, he's adjusted his course slightly and is self-publishing most of his books, but has a contract with a mid-sized traditional publisher for others. His mantra over the years has been to do what makes sense at the time, adjust course when something to further your career comes along.

Joe can be brash, combative, and some would say insulting. He writes what he thinks without apology or caveat. For some possibly twisted reason, I find blunt advice from people who don't pull their punches to be very inspirational. I believe part of the reason I'm drawn to this kind of advice is because deep inside, I know these things, and it's as if some other part of myself is shouting at me — *This is what's true and you're not paying attention. Get your act together once and for all!*

Here are two handfuls of his advice that I should consider tattooing on the inside of my wrist.

I hope they'll inspire you as well.

1. This [building a career as a novelist] is a marathon, not a sprint. (Certainly not original but surprisingly difficult to remember.)

2. When you're learning how to walk, you don't take

classes. You don't read how-to books. You don't pay experts to help you or do it for you. You just keep falling until you learn on your own.

3. Hard work trumps talent. Persistence trumps inspiration. Humility trumps ego.

4. The experts don't know everything, and they might not know what's right for you. (Including Joe, he's quick to add)

5. Stop Googling yourself. (Who, me??!)

6. Write when you can. Finish what your start. Edit what you finish. Self-publish. Repeat.

7. If you're not in love with the sound of your own voice, how can you expect anyone else to ever be?

8. Knowing you're not original is the first step in becoming unique.

9. There should only be a few people in your life whose opinion matters. The opinions of everyone else do not.

10. If you're reading this blog, you aren't writing. Get back to work.

Go read the rest. It might be worth revisiting every month. I know I do.

What I know

In addition to and in imitation of Joe's list, here's what I know:

- *Fiction* is a fiction writer's platform.
- Social media does not sell books — it is not a platform. It is a collection of communication and branding tools.
- I can't control word of mouth, and that's the only thing that brings new readers on a long-term, consistent basis.
- Agents do not negotiate good contracts, and they take a cut of all profits for minimal work.
- For those in the early stages of their careers, traditional publishing, in 2018 and beyond, is not the best bet for writers who want to earn a living with their fiction.
- There are tens of millions of readers with varying tastes.
- Being true to my voice is the ***only*** way to become consistently successful — be the trend others chase.
- Persistence matters.

Shameless

"Imagine the story you want to read, then shamelessly write it."
— JD Salinger

"Everyone has talent. What's rare is the courage to follow it to the dark places where it leads." — Erica Jong

It's so easy to lift your fingers from the keys, staring in horror at the story unfolding in your imagination, wondering where this stuff came from. If you have the courage to get past that, in come the worries about marketability and genre and readers and tropes you've failed to adhere to and comparing to other books which are not your books. It's easy to stare at this creation and question its value and pick it apart with more vicious gouges than any critic might inflict.

And then there are the critics.

Once you start selling books, and reviews show up the self-doubt blooms. A review that echoes what you yourself worried about is devastating. As if the reader had crawled inside your brain. But then, what to do with those reviews that say the exact opposite of one another? And I mean exact.

The title of one says — **Very Disappointing** and two reviews down is a heading that proclaims — **Never Disappoints**.

Reading reviews, listening to critics does not help you write shamelessly. And shamelessly means: *without* "a painful feeling of humiliation or distress caused by the consciousness of wrong or foolish behavior." Shameless means to write what passes through your mind without inspecting it for flaws, without considering how others will take it, without pulling punches, without revising to some false idea of not looking like a dark, emotional, unstable, violent [fill in the blank] person.

Writing shamelessly means that if your story might offend or upset or enrage or elicit dislike or mockery or any number of horrible individual and societal reactions, you write it anyway.

Does everyone have talent as Ms. Jong asserts? I don't know. But the courage to follow to a dark place can be difficult to access. Some are born with that courage. Some seem born with a lack of concern for what others think of them or anything they do. Some are raised into that mindset. Others have to wrestle and subdue strong voices to get there.

Most, and that includes me with an uppercase M, are very much concerned. And the entire nature of doing anything artistic, once you're past the phase of doing it for the pure creative pleasure and self-satisfaction, means finding others who might be touched or moved by what you've brought into the world.

And when you do that, those voices enter the room, enter your mind, and the battle begins.

I'm not good enough.

My stories are trite.

My voice is derivative.

My characters don't resonate.

My plots aren't what others expect…

Add to this the fact that no creative work ever comes out as you imagined. Never. The very act of exiting your brain changes it. Physical reality changes it, coming from the dark corners of your mind to the light of day makes it look different, even if it didn't *change* fundamentally.

If you're not writing that story growing inside of *your* imagination or following *your* talent to those dark places, you have nothing to offer. Because all an artist has is her story or painting, poem or sculpture or film, the one that wants to come out into the daylight.

Does every human being truly have a natural aptitude for telling a story? Yes, because we tell stories every day of our lives. Every single one of us — *Guess what happened to me? You won't believe what I saw...*

Hacks

This term has plagued me for years. Somewhere along the way, I absorbed the belief that *prolific* often meant *hack*. Self-published writers are encouraged to publish several novels a year in order to feed a thirsty market.

But I was afraid to write too many novels. Wouldn't writing several novels a year mean I was *cranking them out*? That I was a *hack*? Finally, one day, I wandered over to the dictionary sitting among my apps. All writers know, you know — the dictionary clarifies things. In fact, one of the ways I gained executive respect in my day job was through the dictionary.

In marketing, people talked constantly about providing *factoids* for marketing brochures and web pages, press releases and customer presentations. One day, it occurred to me I didn't really know precisely what the word meant. It turned out, I didn't know at all. Neither did anyone else. Surprisingly, shockingly, it means this: *An assumption or speculation that is reported and repeated so often that it becomes accepted as fact.*

In fact, it meant the opposite of what people wanted to communicate when they used the term. When I informed my manager of this, she was stunned, and immediately passed it on to everyone she spoke with. They, in turn, were stunned at their foolish repetition of a word they thought they knew and their mindless assumption repeated so often, the meaning was accepted...as fact.

I'd thought of a hack as someone who writes too fast and therefore, not very well.

A hack churns out books.

A hack isn't thoughtful in her writing.

A book that isn't labored over for years is written by a hack.

Layered in the vague and superficial term, *too fast*, is the emphasis on not enough workshopping and edits and crafting of language. Not enough throwing away of one's work and re-crafting it from the start. Not enough input from others and not enough search for perfection, never concerned that the very perfection one seeks might be drowning out all originality.

In fact, the term hack refers to "a writer or journalist producing dull, unoriginal work".

How special that writers are given our own customized insult.

In the common perceptions, writing too fast, making use of minimal editorial input and critique and suggestions for change risks turning an original writer into a hack.

Instead, like factoid, it's the opposite. Work is dull and unoriginal when it's trying to please too many people, when it's trying to conform to others' expectations, when the life of a writer's unique voice is polished and edited out of the story.

I've already given the example of reviews that contradict each other. The same problem exists with all editorial feedback. One beta reader will salivate over a scene while another advises cutting it altogether. One will say the story drags, another that it's fast-paced. One will deem the characters cardboard, and another will fall in love with a character who came to life.

Writing fast, producing more than one novel a year, does not make a writer a hack as is often tossed at indie writers by the traditional publishing world like a handful of mud or a rotten tomato. Rather, over-thinking and over-writing and too much revision dulls the original shine.

My voice is original when my brain flies without the censorship of other voices. When I workshop and over edit, the work loses its shine. So in truth, a hack is someone trying too hard to be literary, trying too hard to meet market conventions of what's selling.

WHAT'S HOLDING YOU BACK?

Fear

Writing is terrifying.

In his book, *The Courage to Write*, Ralph Keyes says writing is like dancing naked on a table in a restaurant. It's been years since I read that statement. I saw the truth in it, but I thought I had an end run around it. I write fiction. I can hide myself behind characters, bury myself beneath made-up stories. There's no risk. There's nothing to be afraid of. I don't have to expose myself or be vulnerable in any way whatsoever.

It wasn't until I was writing this book that I realized how wrong I was, once again, proving I'm a slow learner.

But in some ways, fiction exposes the writer more than non-fiction does. [And I so shrink from exposure that I originally wrote the previous sentence as — *fiction exposes me more*, and then I edited it…distancing myself]. I let very few people see what's inside of me. I don't want people to know how I feel, what scares me, what makes me hurt. I don't want them to know when I feel insecure or embarrassed or jealous. I don't know where this comes from. Maybe it's common. It's not something I discuss with more than two or three people. Possibly, this is a facet of being an introvert. But for the most part, it doesn't matter what the cause is or how common it is. It's my instinct to keep things close.

I was raised to speak only what's polite. In fact, I was explicitly instructed — *If you can't say something nice, don't say anything at all*.

Many emotions on the human scale of feelings are not nice. Sylvia Plath insisted that everything is "writeable about if you have the outgoing guts to do it". I suppose the book mentioned a moment ago was titled *The Courage to Write* for obvious reasons.

I've had to labor relentlessly, over the years, to ignore the censor that makes herself known at every turn. I grew up before the computer age. Once the ability to write journals in a document on my laptop became possible, instead of in the open and easily exposed pages of a notebook, I was in heaven. I was given password protection. I could write freely without that voice in the back of my mind whispering constantly, and occasionally screaming — *Don't say that! Don't use that word, don't make that observation, don't allow your character to do that thing!! Danger! People will know those thoughts passed through your head.*

It's impossible to write a novel, to writing anything at all, if that voice is in charge. So I've wrestled in the mud every day, trying to silence that voice. I've tried not to wonder too much why someone who is so private has chosen a path through the world that requires her to be an exhibitionist. To dance naked on a table.

The funny thing about writing fiction, once that censor is gagged, is that people tend to think they see things from my life in my work, but more often than not, they misread and misinterpret. Those scenes and interior monologues that required a great deal of courage and superhuman strength to write past the censor go unnoticed. Casual passages that did not threaten my fear of self-exposure are seen as very *telling*.

In some ways that's worse. Family and friends pinpoint a character and think it's based on a particular individual and draw conclusions about my view of that individual. One hundred percent of the time, so far, they've been wrong. Yet, there's still a terrible self-revelation. The fear of being misinterpreted, of being thought you're something you are not, or being seen for what you are and shunned.

Even though they get the characters wrong, there's still all those emotions. All those dark and scary things I feel that I've spent a lifetime keeping inside except for a handful of people closest to me. Less than a handful.

And now I'm going to write those things down! I'm going to publish those things that come from inside of me and invite the entire English-speaking world to have a peek inside!

Another truism from my childhood — *Never put in writing something you don't want the whole world to know.* Indeed. Yet, what does a writer do? Puts the inside of her mind out there for the whole world to see.

Despite the fear, I'm going to keep digging into those scary, sensitive feelings. I'm going to work for hours every day to make sure they are as crisp and clear and vivid and real as I can make them. I'm not just going to expose my feelings to the world, I'm going to illustrate them to the very best of my ability. I'm going to work long and hard and do my best to make absolutely sure they see every glittering facet.

It's terrifying. And half the time, when I'm supposed to be writing, and I'm not, it's because that censorial voice is screaming at a volume so loud it's beyond my range of hearing, nothing but a high pitched tone that freezes me, warning me not to take the risk.

What are you afraid of?

The Killer in Your Head

Aside from what I've written already on the topic of fear and self-doubt and censorship, there's more!

I believe the critical voice is a thing. At times, it can have the strength and volume of an actual entity, the old meme of the tiny devil sitting on your shoulder with unfettered access to your ear, leading directly to your mind.

It's common knowledge that critical voice is a force that writers, all artists, need to be aware of and work to get under control, or rather, silence. The critical voice is the embodiment of the parental voice trying to protect a child from pain. *If you touch the stove, you'll get burned.* It protects from secondary sources of physical pain — *If you sleep all morning and are late for work, you'll lose your job and starve.* And more subtle — *If you speak the unvarnished truth, people will shun you, and you'll experience emotional pain.* The irony of holding one's tongue is that vulnerability through truth-telling is what connects the human race. Like anything, there's a balance, but letting that over-protective voice suggest that you must hold back, urging you not to give your imagination and observations of the world free reign, is death to fiction.

When I was in my mid-thirties, a friend of my parents, a university professor (which endowed his voice with greater authority), told me he didn't read fiction. He liked to read about things that were *true*. I was too polite to argue. That's what I thought at the time. Now I know, I was too cowed by that voice of *authority*, the framework I grew up with that insisted one did not argue about *truth* with an elder, with a *professor*!

Inside my head, my four-year-old self was screaming like a naughty, badly behaved, disrespectful little girl — *Fiction carries more truth than anything you'll ever read in a history book.* I know. I studied history. History is interpretation, it's selective inclusion of what the historian deems important. It's propaganda. It's secrets that get left out, stories that are ignored until decades, often centuries, later. As they say, history is written by the victor. History is written by those in power.

Fiction is truth and telling the truth is hard. At least it was for me. It meant exposure, it meant the possibility of rejection and criticism and ridicule.

After parental safe-keeping is firmly embedded in the subconscious and the child moves out into society, the critical voice makes new friends. Schoolteachers.

That's not how it's done.

That's the wrong answer.

Sit still.

That's not how you do it.

Quiet down.

The consequence of not obeying is pain in some form — bad grades bringing further pain in the form of parental disapproval or restrictions, threats of a doomed future.

Classmates join the party.

Loser. Tattletale. You're too skinny, fat, stupid, smart. You can't play with us. Easy out. These are the clothes that everyone is wearing. And those are the minor criticisms. They don't even come close to outright bullying. It's far, far worse for some.

My critical voice and I danced a dance of madness for too long, and if I think about life beyond writing fiction, it's probably been a lifelong affair that encompassed my entire being, starting with — *You're too skinny.* What I wouldn't give to hear that insult now.

Early on when I was learning about the craft of fiction, I read about the critical voice. The way to overcome that voice was the *shitty first draft* — write without judging the words or ideas. Judgement should be saved for editing. And then, after years of practice, as a writer becomes more adept, the shitty first draft isn't always all that shitty. The clean-up becomes easier, less like demolition and more like using a hand vacuum.

In *Writing Down the Bones*, Natalie Goldberg urges writers to ignore margins and punctuation and spelling. Write without stopping. It breaks past that critical voice. Even if you write the same slop over and over, even if it's dull as cement, keep the words flowing and eventually, good things will be unearthed.

I read about taming the Inner Critic. I did exercises to overcome my critical voice. For a while, I had a ceramic crocodile with pink wings sitting in my writing space. It leered at me from the bookcase — my own personal, customized critical voice trying to tear at me with sharp teeth, flying in when least expected.

I knew the truth of shitty first drafts and writing fast. I knew that when I wrote without censoring myself, I wrote good stories. The act of discovering what I was thinking and what I wanted to say and the characters making their voices heard through my fingers was like magic. Once every ten days.

During the nine days in between, I stared at walls, read blogs, played games on my phone.

I read more books that gave insight on overcoming the critical voice: *The War of Art* and *Turning Pro* by Stephen Pressfield.

Slowly, month by month, I became more aware of that Voice. I thought.

But it was still there. The Voice was softer, and that was worse. I wasn't fully conscious of its presence, of its nasty words.

When I wrote, I had a bad habit of stopping every 150-200 words, skipping over to my spreadsheet to add up my word count, seeing how close I was getting to the goal. Not always. But often. Most days. For a few minutes, I'd get lost in the story, and then I'd pause. Add up words. Check email. Surf the web. Play a game.

I was only half aware I was doing this.

In one of those inexplicable flashes of insight, I realized that this constant stopping to calculate and distract myself was the critical voice. Softer than a whisper, it was right there, and I'd never noticed. All my reading about it and awareness of it had forced it to burrow deeper into my mind. Those pauses? They came from a barely audible, barely articulated feeling…

You've started three sentences in a row with a proper noun.

No one talks like that.

Your characters drink too much wine.

That character does nothing but walk across the room.

That sounds silly.

That's heavy-handed.

This is boring.

You have no idea where this story is going, and it's going nowhere.

It went on and on and on. Every few hundred words there was another thing I was doing "wrong".

Finally, I came up with a plan. I would keep my laptop journal open at all times. Each time I paused, I asked myself what I was thinking and wrote it down. Cumbersome? A little. Distracting? Not as distracting as stopping writing, going to retrieve my phone to check Facebook or Twitter or email or the weather or Goodreads or KBoards or my sales rank.

Eventually, I moved to another trick that's still working well. I set a timer for eleven minutes, and I'm not allowed to lift my fingers off the keyboard for those eleven minutes. It's essentially Natalie Goldberg's guidance to *keep your hand moving*.

What did your critical voice say the last time you wrote? What is it saying right now?

INDIE & TRADITIONAL

Third-guessing

There's nothing like making a decision, affirming it by investing enormous amounts of time and some money, celebrating it, then second-guessing. And third-guessing, and fourth…

I was raised on the stories of the Bible. In one story, severe punishment is inflicted upon a woman who looks back at the life she's leaving behind. As a result of her lack of commitment, she's turned into a pillar of salt. Maybe that's why there were so many tears as I tried to get a stable footing in the slick mud of indie publishing. I was turning to salt.

Every time an agent posted a blog about the *tsunami of crap*, the *delusional writer impatience*, the *inevitable career destruction* that was self-publishing, I cringed. (Yes, I *still* read their blogs, for years after making the self-publishing decision. Even today, from time to time, I'm curious what their view of the publishing industry looks like. What can I say…addictions have a death grip and are very, very difficult to break.)

When I read their chastising cries, I worried. I counted ebooks listed in my genre on Amazon. I compared my covers and my interiors and the quality of the paper on my paperbacks and worried. And I knew they weren't talking about the weight of paper or the flexibility of a cover, they were talking about the story, the language, the words.

From perusing the look-inside samples, I knew there was some truth to their claim that many people who hadn't yet developed the skills to engage and tell a good story were publishing books. Anyone can publish a book now. In the early days of ebook self-publishing, many of the indie novels were full of grammatical errors and typos, the stories were dull and sometimes, incomprehensible. If not that, they were simplistic and filled with information dumps and description rather than story-telling. I don't know if that's still the case, I finally, finally,

FINALLY stopped comparing. (Addictions can be broken after all.)

It became clear why editors and agents had been saying for years they can tell within the first five pages, the first page, the first paragraph whether someone can write. Was this the company I was keeping? Writers deluded into thinking the first story they wrote, the first draft, was so incredibly compelling they published it without feedback or editorial oversight? I clung to my handful of traditionally published short stories like a flotation device in the middle of the Pacific Ocean. Yes, I could write. Editors had said I could tell a story. They enjoyed the stories enough to pay me. But still, I worried. Those were short stories, novels are different.

And soon, I found myself writing about ghosts. Had I really read enough horror literature to qualify me to tell a solid ghost story that wasn't derivative?

And my novels. The characters were unlikable! I scrutinized my reviews and managed to extract and highlight the negative comment from every single good review. When a review suggested I needed an editor, I took to my virtual bed for days, despairing that I was a fool for choosing to do this myself, without a publishing company and its validation and resources behind me.

Maybe I wasn't good enough. Maybe I hadn't been vetted after all. At the same time, maybe it didn't even matter, because my books were lost in a sea of self-published fiction that poured daily through the gates of Amazon and other ebook stores.

Maybe I'd made a mistake. I should have gone the traditional route, tried longer and harder to find an agent, gained the third-party validation that my novels had market potential.

Yet, I kept going. I can't even say why. I think deep inside, something told me that those were false fears and that yes, my publishing credits proved I did know how to write. There were enough badly written, poorly edited books with terrible covers coming out of the big publishing houses that my gut told me to hang on.

Every time *Five Essential Tips for Book Marketing* or *Seven Steps* to *Promote Your Novel* or *Ten Whatever* popped into my inbox, I launched a new plan. Platform was critical. Engaging on social media while never, ever, ever over-tweeting your books was the key to visibility. I traded Facebook page likes with other indie authors. I posted updates, and no one responded. I tweeted. I found followers. I re-tweeted. Occasionally I promoted a book. The tweets disappeared like a grain of sand into the Amazon River.

Then the looking back began anew. I should have exhausted every avenue to find an agent, a publisher, a multi-national corporation with a marketing team and a publicist. Not that ninety-percent of debut writers receive those things, but surely there would be *something*. Other writers who were fleeing traditional publishing insisted that no, new writers did not get that support. But still. Maybe I'd made a mistake. I had no platform. I published flash fiction. I believed that could be a platform. But it didn't seem to be a platform.

Every time there was a marketing splash that only a Big Five publisher can pull off, I collapsed in despair. I followed the careers of writers I knew who were slogging down that road. Some were doing okay, some not so okay, some were disappearing, no new books published for years, and some were superstars.

I'd spent so much time and energy and heart following the requirements of the publishing industry, most of which had been communicated via literary agents. More importantly, I'd spent that time buying hook, line, and sinker into the belief system that self-published writers were pathetic, crap writers, and borderline mentally ill. Seriously.

Finally, I'm no longer looking back. I haven't read an agent's blog in months. I'm not sure I've read one this year. I've accepted my life as borderline mentally ill and am happy there.

No difference

The day-to-day and year-to-year experience of indie publishing are, nearly the same as traditional publishing. It took me years to come to that realization and belief.

Those first years, waiting to find an audience weren't all that different. I released a book and had a few sales. I wrote another book. In traditional publishing, you write a novel and query an agent. While you query, you start writing a second novel. You may finish that one. You find an agent. You write another novel while she submits to publishers. You finish that novel, you sign a contract. Your book will be out in eighteen months. Now you are starting, possibly, your *fourth* novel.

Except for the rare exceptions, writers on both paths need to do a tremendous amount of waiting.

While you're stalking agents, you're building the elusive, *essential* platform. You're tweeting with other writers. You're writing a blog, maybe. You're developing a Facebook page and adding content to your website. You're diligent and dedicated because you're fully aware that once a publisher accepts your manuscript, you'll be instructed to do these things. In fact, you're painfully aware that agents and publishers are looking at your social media footprint even as they read your query letter, an excerpt from your novel.

Whether your novels are self- or traditionally-published, you'll receive negative reviews. You'll receive reviews that wonder why your editor is missing in action. You'll receive reviews that say you can't write, your book is predictable or any number of other criticisms. You'll find fans and marvel with gratitude you can't express.

Whether you're doing it yourself or through a huge corporation, you need to build an audience. In fact, part of what's not working in traditional publishing in 2018 as I write this is that new writers with signed contracts in hand aren't given a chance to build an audience. Success is expected out of the gate, and poor sales numbers (meaning sales numbers below what was forecast based on guesswork and gut feelings) usually means the end of your contract with that publisher. *Do not pass Go, do not collect two hundred dollars.*

Whether or not you have a team of so-called experts providing input into your story or a few hand-picked friends, you'll battle self-doubt. Facing the blank screen is a battle with self-doubt. Negative reviews invite a skirmish of self-doubt. A trickle of sales invites the same.

At their core, self-publishing and traditional publishing are the same.

But then, there are the differences.

Creative control. The ability to publish at the pace you write, not force-fit into someone else's schedule. A significantly greater percentage of the profit from your work.

Creative control means you can write the story that excites you without being told there's "no market". Creative control means you can commission a cover design that you feel reflects and sells your story, not something obscure that sinks the book because no one is drawn to the visual impression when it's the size of your thumb. Creative control means doing it yourself, following your vision.

It's terrifying and incredibly satisfying.

Yesteryear

In an online conversation between Pulitzer Prize winner, Richard Russo and the Executive Director of the Author's Guild, Paul Aiken, Barry Eisler jumped in to direct their attention to the realities of the publishing industry. Barry is the traditionally published author of the John Rain series and gained a lot of attention when he turned down a $500,000 contract to self-publish his fiction.

This conversation took place in 2014.

Richard Russo: When I was a young writer there were many newspapers that reviewed lots of books. Young writers also got sent on book tours, even when those tours lost money. There was much more money for advertising. Over time, writers could find an audience, not through algorithms but through dedicated local booksellers. It's harder, much harder today, and writers who haven't made a name for themselves face a much more difficult time of it for all kinds of reasons. Honestly, I don't know if I could do now what I did then.

...

Richard Russo: The role of publishers will become clear as traditional publishers disappear. The role of the publisher has always been to nurture the writer. My early books were all published well, but didn't sell in large numbers. Other bestsellers allowed my publisher to carry me until I could pay my own way. And I've had two of the best editors in the business, who have made every book better, and not by a little. You notice when books aren't edited well.

Paul Aiken: I've followed this closely. The publisher's role has traditionally been partly a venture capital role — funding the author's work. It's a critical function, especially for new authors. That doesn't mean there shouldn't be other means to reach readers. Amazon's done a good job at providing those.

Barry Eisler: They're talking about twenty or more years ago — and not the last decade or so.

I haven't heard new and unknown authors, let alone a lot of mid-listers, talk about how they believed their editors and publishers were helping to build their career in a very long time. Advances are down, getting subsequent books published if previous ones sold poorly is more difficult, and book tours are pretty much reserved for those whose books are proven sellers.

And sorry, but badly edited books have been released by traditional publishing for easily a century but especially the past several decades — a trend that has grown more pervasive since the 1980s. I'll say that traditional publishing probably catches more typos or outright grammar mistakes. But issues with pacing, clumsy dialogue, thin and undeveloped characters, bad plotting, etc. regularly flow out. Some of it becomes bestsellers — since none of those things have ever been an impediment to appeal.

I just don't understand waxing nostalgic about a past that's past.

Rather than saying what traditional publishing used to do how about defending what they do now?

...

I include this because many of the benefits of traditional publishing are indeed relics of twenty, closer to thirty years ago. Richard Russo's first novel was published in 1986. He won the Pulitzer Prize in 2002. His experiences are indeed ancient history in the accelerating timeline of digital advancement.

All the things Richard Russo mentioned are things that I, and many other writers, wanted and expected. An editor at a legacy publishing company would fall in love with my voice. She would edit my work brilliantly, and their talented artist would provide a breath-taking cover. The book would be promoted to bookstore owners and reviewed in print media. The publisher would send me on book tours (at their expense, of course) and arrange radio interviews.

Most of that is laughably archaic in 2018. Print media is rare, and people under forty who get their information from it are rarer still. Radio has been displaced by streaming. And these marketing benefits delivered by traditional publishing companies have evaporated. People can filter their worlds to their own advertising-free playlists and customized news feeds. But even with those not insignificant hurdles, there are still opportunities to market your work. Opportunities that you're now required to develop on your own no matter who publishes your work.

And those dreams of yesteryear are as unrealistic as the expectation that millions of people will sit down to watch the pilot episode of a new TV show at the same moment in time. Listening to writers whose careers came of age in a different era is downright detrimental to writers now. A writer who doesn't sell well out of the gate is not likely to get a second chance.

Self-publishing is filled with second chances. And third chances.

SALES ADDICT

Cheating

In the past eight years, I believe I've checked sales and Amazon sales ranks close to ten thousand times. Malcolm Gladwell, author of *Outliers*, offered anecdotal evidence that the key to achieving world-class expertise is gained through investing ten thousand hours into an artistic, business, or sports pursuit. I don't think he meant ten thousand hours checking the status of a number over which you have absolutely no control.

On the days when I'd scheduled special promotions, I checked hourly, half hourly. Every ten minutes!

Many times I engaged my husband to help me stop this destructive, soul-destroying, time-wasting habit. This obsession. It's the addiction of the digital age — every second of every day there is new information to be had somewhere. A new tweet, a new blog post, a crime, a political fight, terrorism, scandal, a friend's new photo on Facebook, a witty comment about life, the world, people, politics…a discussion about indies vs. traditionals, a new book-marketing technique, a new rumor.

I could spend every moment of my life clicking refresh and getting a new jolt to my brain. It's as addictive as crack. Not that I know how addictive crack is, but I'm told it is. It's as addictive as smoking cigarettes. During college, I smoked, and it was absolutely addictive. Nicotine aside, the ritual of lighting and taking that first inhale, the pleasure of watching soft, gentle, calming smoke flow out of your lips…It took me years to quell the desire. I quit when I was twenty and continued to cheat for a good four or five years after, when I was at a party, when others were smoking, I couldn't resist.

And maybe that's the lure of social media. Others are doing it. There's a whole world out there, and I might miss an important part. Life will pass me by. It's even a named *thing* — FOMO, Fear Of Missing Out.

It's appropriate to categorize the addiction to checking sales the same way. New information! A new reader! Will s/he become a fan? A change in my sales rank, another few dollars in my account. Several ebook stores to look at. If nothing's happening at this one, maybe something's happening there. Little maps displaying where my readers are. Blue bars, gold bars, graph lines. The seductive slide as the screen refreshes and the bar grows before your eyes.

It was exhausting, and it created an emotional tornado. At one point, I decided I'd only check sales once a week. My husband and I would sit at the desk together on Sunday mornings. Then came a few weeks with no sales at all. It was too depressing. I would check once a month. That was the new plan. It was rational and sane. I'd put one seashell at the feet of my statue depicting the Egyptian god of writing. (Yes, I'm often and easily drawn into rituals and icons and talismans.) Each day I focused on writing and not on sales, I'd place the polished white shell fragment at the wooden feet of this ancient god.

Except, I cheated.

I'll just check today, so I can track the Amazon sales rank of my promotional freebies. That feels good, most of the time. Except when the rank falls, meaning my number of downloads, of potential new readers, has slipped. And checking ~~will~~ might lead me to look at sales.

Yes! That's better. My free rank slipped, but it's okay because maybe I sold some books. I did! Woo-hoo. Ecstasy! Elation! Happy dance and my heart exploding with joy.

Always trying to be honest with myself and my ever-new goals and plans and rules, I'd scoop up all the seashells and return them to the jar, again, defeated and annoyed with myself.

When we began using Amazon Ads, and steady sales followed, we had to check daily to stay on top of ad spending, making adjustments to the bids or writing new ads. But sales still fluctuate wildly, and the desire to cheat is as intense as ever. I played games to stop my bad habit, I tried forming new habits to replace it, I went several days with only the single check. But then, it was as if a tsunami overtook me and I was unable to control the forces driving me, opening the Amazon publishing window, clicking the refresh button like a mad monkey. I can launch the window by typing K and D in the URL box. My browser knows.

It's almost worse when sales are going well. The thrill of seeing them increase every time I look is even more addictive. But then, that surge stalls and I go back to hitting that button with increasing despair. I turn off internet access to stop myself and then end up leaving my writing room to pick up my phone. I go to the Book Report tool looking at sales or to an Amazon page to check a book's rank. It's exhausting and a wild roller coaster of elation and despair.

A new day is coming. Today, for sure, I promise — cross my heart and hope to die — I will go for twenty-four hours without cheating. I know I can do it. Can you?

Is There An Audience?

Is there an audience for my fiction?

A writer seeking a traditional publishing contract asks this question knowing she'll receive the answer when an agent signs her on, when a publishing house makes an offer. When the "experts" ~~know~~ believe that a book has market potential, they put their time, reputation, and money on the line.

For a self-published writer, the question is trickier, messier, and at first, never-ending.

My sister is an artist — she paints stunning, thought-provoking, moving abstracts. In a class she took about marketing your work to galleries, the instructor stated in no uncertain terms that there is an audience for every painter. He truly believes this. He devotes his time and expertise to helping visual artists find theirs. He believes that marketing correctly and being persistent and thorough will enable his students to find that audience.

I like his enthusiasm, I love his affirmation and support. I'm not sure whether or not I agree, but I want very much to agree.

I didn't hear his wisdom until recently, and for years, I wondered whether there was an audience for my kind of fiction. I twisted myself into knots thinking about this, asking this question of myself and my husband, over and over with such intensity and frequency I cringe thinking about it now.

As I've mentioned before, I started out thinking I wanted to write literary fiction. When I uncovered my affinity for crime and slowly made my way to exploring the psychological forces that lead "normal" people to commit crimes, I found myself without a well-tailored genre to shove my arms and shoulders into.

Because my books have characters that are deemed unlikable, would anyone want to read about them? They're not people you necessarily want to root for like readers do for the threatened heroines of most thrillers or the zealous, avenge-the-victim-at-all-costs law enforcement personnel in suspense novels. I love my characters, but would anyone else?

I'm fascinated by human behavior, and especially troublesome and neurotic human behavior. I love my characters because they struggle. They do what they have to do, what they're compelled to do. They're fighting for their psychological lives. But were there any readers who would feel the same way?

Writing groups and peers and countless books on the craft of fiction tell me readers want characters they can root for, cheer for, admire, and identify with on all levels.

The murders in my stories most often happen at the end of the story, which tells the events that lead to the crime. Suspense and thriller novels most often have the crime up front. Pacing in psychological suspense is calmer. Mental activity, rather than physical action, drives my stories. Tension in most psychological suspense stories builds gradually. The stories have a claustrophobic feel.

Novels of psychological suspense create worlds of unease and potential disaster in which characters explore their options and their obsessions, while the reader observes from the outside. In this way, they fit firmly in the genres that appeal to the intellect. Masters of the genre create disturbing tales of unbalanced minds, and as we readers observe in morbid fascination, we are pulled into their nightmare worlds. These are puzzles that explore the mind and its inner workings in troubling tales of heart-racing suspense.

This is how the genre is often described, yet not how it typically plays out in current market trends, especially in the

American fiction market.

Labeling a book a psychological thriller — the only primary category for my books —draws many readers who are looking for something entirely different from what I write.

As in Literary Fiction (which may be the reason my fascination with the motivations behind crime merged with my attraction to literary fiction), the endings of psychological suspense stories may be unresolved or carry some ambiguity. They are stories that, like literary fiction, close a door but open a window. The lingering of unanswered questions adds to the unease generated by the story. The writer raises troubling issues, creates disturbed and disturbing characters, and then leaves the reader to wonder at the outcome.

But are these the type of stories that sell enough books to provide a living for a writer?

During those years when I was selling a handful of books a month, I wasn't at all sure there was an audience. When reviews came in, and my average struggled to pull itself to three-and-a-half stars in some cases, I feared the audience didn't exist.

When the "read-through" that everyone told me was critical to the success of a series was nowhere near the seventy to eighty percent that indie experts claimed was crucial, I stared at my percentage and agonized over the way my muse seemed to constantly lead me outside of typical genre expectations.

Yet, every time I tried to write something different, something that was more aligned with conventional crime fiction, something that adhered more to expected tropes, I veered off course without even realizing I was doing it. When I saw I'd once again stepped off the path, I was too caught up in where the story was going to have any interest in tossing it all and starting over with an outline.

Now, I think one of the reasons it's taken me so very long to get a steady flow of sales is because my books don't fit into a defined set of expectations. But once readers found them and fell in love with the sociopaths and neurotics, the insecure and vengeful and self-absorbed people that grew in my imagination, I was overjoyed.

Still, I worried. *Was* there an audience, *enough* of an audience to ever realize my dream?

Now, I think I've come to see that my sister's instructor is right. There is an audience for every artist.

The question I'm really asking is — *Is that audience large enough for me to make a living?*

When you think about the seven billion people on the planet, even when you narrow that to the approximately twenty percent who speak English, there's an audience. Helping them find your books is the more challenging part.

Do you believe there's an audience for your work? Try describing your ideal reader. Lots of marketing books advise this, and if you stop thinking about it from a marketing perspective and let your playful side come out, it's quite fun.

CHICKENS & EGGS

The Review Trap

You must have reviews!
  Reviews are critical for selling books!
  Get reviews in advance, so your book hits the ground running!

I can't argue with those statements. The question that plagued me, and thousands of other self-published writers was — *How does one get reviews?* It's the quintessential chicken and egg because there are basically five ways to get reviews, and all of them have to do with finding readers, which reviews are supposed to bring.

1. Pay for them.
  It's been done. It's been exposed, Amazon cracked down, it's still done.
  I listed this first to shock you, and to make a point.
  Secondary to flat-out buying reviews (which I don't have to say is highly unethical and will get your reviews deleted) there are outfits that distribute electronic copies of your book to people who have signed up to review your genre, collecting an administrative fee for their service. The reviewers don't receive any money, and there's a firewall between reviewer and writer. This results in an unbiased review. Some readers might feel compelled by the free book to be kinder, although most aren't. And if they are compelled to pull their punches, they're required to disclose the receipt of a free book which gives future book buyers context.
  I used one of these services for my first two novels and one of my novellas. I received some good reviews through this process, as well as a range of reactions, which is good. I surely did not want the clearly-stacked decks of books with almost all 5-stars, the 4-stars pushing hard on the 5-star heels and nothing else.

Fiction is taste. Some readers will love your novels, some will like them, some will feel *meh*, and some will hate them.

Partially through observing my own book-buying habits, I came to realize that negative reviews are actually a good thing. When a book description interests me, I jump first to the 1- and 2-star reviews. When I read that a protagonist is *too stupid to live*, I pass. When a reader complains about characters she hated because they were too deeply flawed (but smart), I'm all over it!

Cherish the negative reviews, they might be bringing more readers than you realize.

2. Ask Mom and cousin Dave to write a review.

It's been done. It's been exposed, Amazon overzealously cracked down, it's still done.

KBoards has multiple message threads about disappearing reviews that resulted from Amazon's bots determining a "relationship", usually via social media, between writer and reader. Often, that "relationship" is simply a reader who fell in love with a writer's voice.

Aside from the risk of losing the review and a smack from Amazon, I can't imagine doing this. For me, it would be so grossly unsatisfying it wouldn't compensate for any boost in sales. It's exciting to see the review pop up, sure, gratifying to read enthusiastic words about your work, but doesn't the worry creep in moments later? Did she really like the book? Is he afraid of hurting my feelings?

Secondary to this method is swapping reviews with other writers.

Again: Done, exposed, still done. And equally unsatisfying for the same reasons.

3. Solicit book bloggers, especially those who also post their reviews on reader sites like GoodReads and on ebook stores.

This has become increasingly difficult. Many book bloggers won't accept books from independent authors. The ones who do are drowning.

I never pursued this as diligently as I should have. Partially because of my untidy genre fit. In the beginning, I was able to land a handful of reviews from book bloggers. One has since stopped accepting books because she couldn't keep up. One was a multi-reviewer site that closed shop. Two found my books without any solicitation from me. Because my sales were so low at that time, I never saw a bump that I could attribute to those reviews. But the heart of the internet beats forever, so never say never.

Pursuing this might be worthwhile, or not. For me, it was simply an exercise in frustration. Tedious, frustrating work with no measurable results.

4. Give away books and cross your fingers.

The giveaway of paperback copies of my first novel via GoodReads worked well. This was in 2011.Winners are asked to provide a review, but it's not required. I gave away ten books and received about five or six reviews. In my second giveaway the following year, I tripled the number of books I gave and even shipped books to readers in the UK and Australia. The same handful left reviews this time, and some took more than a year.

Shortly after my third giveaway (slow learner, remember?), I discovered that some readers enter giveaways in order to run a side business selling books on eBay. Sure enough, some of my books are for sale on eBay, noting the books are in their "original packaging and signed by the author". Of course there are lots of winners who cherish new books and some who take the time to write a review, but still. Cynical much?

I've also offered local drawings for free paperbacks, asking entrants to sign up for my mailing list. The sign-ups were plentiful, but in the end, those who didn't win forgot about me and never, as far as I know, checked out my books. Since only one or two ever opened my newsletter, I think that's a safe assumption.

Now, there are plenty of opportunities to give away free ebooks in the hope of receiving a review. I've never done this, so can't comment. By the time these options became available, I was done with the giveaway model.

5. Wait.

What? *Wait?!* Patience? ***Wait?!!*** But how long??

The upside of organic reviews is the incredible thrill. That first collection of flash fiction that I used to test the ebook water now has twenty-eight reviews on Amazon and seventy-eight ratings (thirteen reviews) on GoodReads. I never asked for a single one. They just came. The book was free at the Amazon US store for several years which helped somewhat. Slowly, the reviews came in. I loved knowing that someone downloaded that little book, read it, and enjoyed it (or disliked it) enough to make a comment.

Gradually, as more readers have discovered my work, reviews and GR ratings have come in greater quantities and more frequently. More often than not, there are only stars on GoodReads, but I'm excited about every single one.

Sometimes readers are beyond succinct — *Well written. Different. Great read. Too many characters, difficult to follow. Good storyline. I just didn't care for it. Great reading.* But I cherish every word.

It's the stuff of dreams to know that someone read my blurb, purchased my novel (or downloaded in Kindle Unlimited) read it, and was motivated to respond. Even the ones who hated the book.

You can't buy that.

Do reviews sell books? Do people avoid buying books because there are no reviews? It's tempting to think armloads of 4- and 5-star reviews will help readers discover and choose your books. Reviews definitely aid Amazon's algorithms in making your books more visible. But I've seen no evidence in my fiction shelves that reviews actually *sell* books, or prevent sales.

As of this writing, I have one book that has sold approximately 750 copies in 2018 alone (about half of those sales are KU downloads). It does not have any reviews on Amazon. For two years, my best selling novel had the lowest rating average of all my books, barely keeping its head above water with a 3.1-star average.

Prowling through the pages of Amazon, I've seen a lot of books with thirty to forty reviews, often averaging well over four stars. Yet according to sales to ranking estimates, even in the first year of life, the book is only selling 1-2 copies a month.

I have no evidence for this, but my feeling, after obsessing, and I do mean *obsessing*, and freaking out over reviews and the lack thereof for more years than I want to think about, that the egg comes first and the chicken follows. Through marketing of one kind or another, readers slowly find and read your books. Then a few more, and a few more. And some write reviews.

Veering back to the previous chapter for a moment, my books spent years with few to no reviews. Some still linger in that no-man's land. I worried incessantly that without readers who were passionate about my work, who were excited enough about my stories to leave a review, there wasn't an audience for my unconventional stories, and while I'm at it, my writing style, which features an abundance of sentence fragments and probably too many run-ons.

I complained regularly to anyone who would listen, or pretend to, that the reviews I did have showed no "passion", that if there wasn't a core group of readers who loved, who adored my books, I would never succeed as a novelist. I wept. I compared my reviews to others. I managed to read every single 5-star review and ferret out the single sentence or phrase that was less than glowing.

When those glowing, fanatical reviews did start coming in, the elation was almost too much to bear. Every time I read one, I feel honored and humbled and incredibly grateful. I'm in awe. I sat in my tiny room and followed my imagination where it led. My words entered the mind of another and provided entertainment and satisfaction and a thirst for more.

It was so worth the wait.

Most marketing books and blogs for indie writers urge a book launch, including advance reviews. Successful writers have a group of loyal readers who read advance copies of a new book and write reviews on publication day. But why does that book start selling immediately? Is it because it has fifteen or fifty reviews? Or is it because it was promoted and looked interesting or is part of a series with a loyal following?

From back in the days when traditional publishing ruled the industry to this moment in time, there are surveys demonstrating that over fifty percent of readers buy books based on either author name recognition or the recommendation of friends. When readers love a writer, they buy every book. Reasons for buying books drop sharply after that, with approximately twenty percent, according to the survey above, buying based on reviews. But this is after they've discovered the book. A review, thirty reviews, will not help readers find your books.

Again: Egg. Chicken.

It's all about the book. And finding those readers who love that book. That voice. Your voice. Because then your book appears on that wonderful sixty-eight percent shelf because of name recognition.

And a final comment about those nasty 1- and 2-stars. *Boring. Hated the characters. Worst book I ever read. Won't buy another from this author. I can't imagine why this was published.* Every writer I love has those reviews. I have those reviews. All writers that I know of have those reviews.

It's still painful and demoralizing. As an antidote, I encourage reading the negative reviews of books you love. If you get a 2-star review and see the same reader gave two stars to *Anna Karenina*, you'll feel pretty damn good.

I've had enough bad reviews now that I can shrug them off (sort off) — *Not my audience.* But it's a very protracted shrug, lasting hours, sometimes twenty-four.

But when one reader gives a low rating and writes that she would *not want* [one of your characters] *taking candid photos of her and her family*, as the femme fatale did in my novel, *The Demise of the Soccer Moms*, you think — exactly! That's how you were supposed to feel.

I'm not saying that reviews don't matter. Of course they help readers make book-buying decisions. Of course critical mass when it comes to reviews gets Amazon's algorithm attention for your books. But in my experience, it's not worth blindly seeking them out. It's worth waiting both for personal satisfaction and because three glowing reviews from your Mom and your Aunt and your Best Friend are not going to move the needle in terms of book sales.

Now that I have a fan base and a newsletter list, I sought advance reviews for my most recent novel. It was a standalone and helped introduce my series fans to my other work. But were sales better than my other book sales during that first month? No. And I won't do it for the next book in my series...those reviews come slowly and organically and the waiting is absolutely worth it.

NetGalley: Boon or Bane?

There are mixed reviews on the value of NetGalley for Indie Authors.

NetGalley is a service that invites book bloggers, publishing industry people, educators, librarians and others to sign up to review books. They state their role and theoretically commit to reviewing a free copy of the books they're drawn to.

Traditional publishers are allowed to vet their reviewers. They can see the history of what a particular reviewer has posted and make decisions about the most favorable reviewers for any given book. As far as I know, this feature is not open to Indie Authors.

Through my membership with the Independent Book Publisher's Association (IBPA), I have a discount on the NetGalley fee. There are also indie groups that sign up as a collective to bear the cost of the rather steep price (over $500 for six months).

It was still expensive, but for the launch of my new series, and not yet having come to the conclusions outlined in the previous chapter on reviews, we decided it was worth the investment to start the book out with a significant number of reviews.

The ebook was posted, and people began requesting it and voting on the cover. I was thrilled. They loved the cover! Hundreds of reviewers wanted to read my book! I had visions of golden stars dancing across my book's page.

Two things made NetGalley a huge disappointment and a

waste of money for me.

Before we invested a chunk of change in NetGalley, we'd read several blogs noting that NetGalley reviewers seem particularly vicious compared to the average reader. But I'd seen lots of reviews citing a free book from NG, and they ran the typical spectrum, so I didn't pay much attention to this. What I didn't factor in was that these were reviews on traditionally published books — in other words, vetted reviewers.

Reviews for my book began to appear. A few 4-stars, a few fives. A sprinkling of threes. Some ones and twos.

The reviews appear first on NetGalley where the author is notified they've been posted. A brief profile of the reviewer appears with the review.

I was excited to see reviews of my book appear start appearing on Amazon and GoodReads and a few review blogs. To cut to the chase — this didn't happen to the extent I'd expected. Out of several hundred people downloading my book, approximately fifty read it and reviewed it. Out of those, about twenty published their reviews in a public forum.

It was beyond frustrating. I'd paid four hundred dollars in part because I understood that the reviewers were committed to posting a review. It was the understanding with which they signed up for NetGalley. I chastised myself for wasting money. Twenty or so reviews aren't awful, but that was not money we had to burn. Worse was the letdown from my excitement over the hundreds of downloads.

Some of those reviews took months to arrive. Part of this was my own naiveté in not thinking it through. Of course, people getting free books are going to have a significant TBR stack. But still, I was frustrated and disappointed.

The second problem was worse. For whatever reason, and maybe this was unique to me, many of the 4- and 5-star reviews were posted on NG but nowhere public. The 1-star and 2-star reactions? They relished writing detailed reviews and spreading them far and wide. I ended up with reviews skewed toward the negative.

Partially it was the book. The protagonist in my series is either loved or loathed. I get a lot of negative reviews of the first book. More than most series.

But partially this was a weird phenomenon in which people who hated the character and hated the book waxed eloquently about what they didn't like. Those who loved the book and couldn't wait for the next in the series hid their adoration behind the locked doors of NetGalley.

Enter at your own risk.

MEANS

Moving On Up

In his book, *Turning Pro*, the sequel to *The War of Art*, Stephen Pressfield notes that it's important to make a mental transition from being a hobbyist to a professional. Even if you aren't yet paid like a professional writer, act like one. It's sort of like the twentieth-century meme — *Dress for the job you want, not the job you have.*

Pressfield identifies the four traits of a Pro as follows:

1. Patient
2. Acts in the face of fear
3. Plays it as it lays
4. Self validates

These struck me because far too often, I'm the polar opposite.

A pro...

Is patient. I want it now. I want superb craft expertise right now. I want the first draft to be brilliant. I want the editing process done now. I want an increase in book sales now. Like most of the human race, I don't like waiting. Does *anyone* like waiting for their desires to be fulfilled?

But every single thing about building a career, especially a career in the arts, requires patience. Things take time. Many things take a long time. Developing skill in writing fiction, absorbing all the hundreds of details of how to develop a character and structure a plot into one's DNA takes years. It just does. Ten thousand hours.

Building an audience takes time. Writing a novel takes time, no matter how fast you write.

Often, time works in your favor. A writer who sees her first novel skyrocket to a bestseller list has nothing else to offer readers who love the book.

Now, when readers find one of my newer books, the novels that languished for years are starting to get picked up. But when I published them, and they sat on the virtual shelf un-read and un-loved, I was terribly impatient for rapid success. Has that made me patient now? Of course not, but at least I have enough distance-perspective (aka time) that can occasionally step back and smile at my antics.

Acts in the face of fear. Writing is an act of courage. We all know some variation of the quote attributed to several writers — *Writing is easy, just open a vein and bleed.*

It's scary to put fears and feelings and vulnerabilities into characters and imprint them onto a screen and sheets of paper and into audio recordings.

Fear freezes our fingers and drives us to the candy buffet of the internet. First, fear keeps us from writing. Fear is what makes us stare out the window or at a blank wall, feeling "blocked". It keeps us from revising because *what if it's still not any "good"*? It keeps us from editing, and we wonder why days pass without any forward movement on our novel. Fear is what keeps us from finding brutally honest beta readers. It keeps us from taking the self-publishing leap.

If you find yourself compelled to dedicating effort to deleting old emails during your writing time, fear has its grip on your mind. If you must shred the paper on top of your shredder right this minute, fear is turning your brain into a master of minutia. When it seems absolutely critical that you immediately stop work to delve deeper into the study of crafting more compelling characters, fear has gone underground and is attacking you with greater subtlety.

The only way to overcome fear is to act. This is said so often, we ignore it. Would that it was so easy as it sounds. Put your fingers on the keyboard and write the next sentence. If the words are lame or boring or grammatically incorrect, think about your character and figure out what she does or says next. Fix the "lame" words later.

Eventually, as your fingers move, fear gives up and takes a short nap. But watch out, when fear wakes up, she's usually on the wrong side of the bed.

Plays it as it lays. This might be my favorite because I like to play golf. I'm not very good, but I keep trying because the satisfaction when I hit a long, smooth shot or putt the ball into that tiny cup is sublime.

In golf, if your ball lands in a sand trap, you hit it. If it's in bounds, but beneath a low-hanging tree branch, you find a way to hit it. If it lands in thick wet grass, you hit it. Very badly, and not very far, but you hit it. You play it as it lays.

Writing is no different. If you missed three days of writing, you start where you are. If there's a chainsaw or car alarm going off outside your window, you put on headphones and hope they block it out. Whatever life is handing you right this minute, that's the place where your writing has to start and find a way to flourish.

Note to self: Wishing your ball or your story was elsewhere is a waste of time.

Self validates. For ages, I asked my husband easily two-hundred-fifty times a year if this or that story was any good, if the latest novel was gripping or well-written, if I could write *at all*. But really, I kept asking because his answer never helped. He would say yes, and I'd either need to hear it again, or I wouldn't believe him.

I needed to trust my own work. I needed to not need his answer.

A cosmetics saleswoman once told me it was imperative that a woman over the age of thirty exfoliates. I still laugh at her hyperbolic use of that word. It is imperative that I feel good about what I create regardless of how many negative reviews or rave reviews the novel or story generates. I'll never get what I want looking to another person to provide that assurance. Honestly, reader feedback has helped. When a stranger loves your books, it does give you a solid boost. But it's not enough, it's short-lived, and it's dangerous to rely on something outside yourself because the external world is in a constant state of flux.

In an interview with Stephen King and Lee Child, both expressed the idea that any given story *is what it is*. Stephen King believes a writer is nothing but a scribe. And Lee Child said an editor once advised him to order the plot differently. He responded, "No, this is how it happened."

There's a balance, of course, between stubborn insistence on worshipping every word you've bled onto the page and needing constant guidance and affirmation. Somewhere in-between is bliss.

This isn't the same as refusing critical feedback on a first draft. It's more about second-guessing, and more about not trusting the process so that at the end, when you've written the best book you can, you still wonder — *Is it any good?* As they say, there lies madness.

I'm still working on this one, but the longer I've been writing fiction, the more I've moved toward the belief that the story as it stands is what my creative mind conceived of. It can always be better, it can always and forever be different, and it will never be perfect. At the same time, it's perfect just as it is.

Dress the Part

So what does it mean to dress the part of the job you want, not the job you have?

I don't know if it still holds, since it was tied to the days of suits and ties, high heels and pencil skirts, but there's still a common belief that there's a kind of positive energy in dress, and acting the part. Although it sounds a bit like magical thinking, there's some benefit to writing as if you're already a self-supporting fiction writer.

Two successful indie authors appear to have adopted that "magical thinking" to some extent. This doesn't mean they don't work relentlessly at their work and improving their craft.

The first is Russell Blake who commented in an interview that his business strategy was to write as though a major publisher were offering him a million dollar contract for each book. This motivated him to work long hours. He attributes some of his success to his rapid release of new fiction.

I thought about this a lot. What would I do differently in my life if I were under contract with a traditional publisher? What would I do if I knew I was going to be paid one million dollars when I delivered my completed novel? Would I write in the evenings when I thought my energy was *too low to be creative*? Absolutely. In fact, I didn't think my energy would be "too low" if that were my reality. Would I spend time surfing the web, scrolling through Twitter and Facebook if that contract was on my desk? Absolutely not!

Hugh Howey said something similar, he allowed himself to daydream before he fell asleep, dreaming that somehow he'd written a dozen novels without his family knowing about it (thus skipping the boring bit of actually writing the novels), and out of nowhere, he became an international bestselling author.

It occurred to me that despite Russell Blake's advice — write a novel every 4-5 weeks (which didn't fit the way I write or the kind of novels I write) — most of what he did was to make sure he treated his writing like a job. He showed up every day and did the work, even when he didn't *feel* creative or have the energy required. He acted the part of the full-time fiction writer before he was earning his living as one. He believes his success is due to publishing a book almost every month, but how much of that was the number of books he published in a short time and how much was it the "luck" that many writers talk about? The "luck" that comes from the notion that "the harder I work, the luckier I get"?

Did his love of writing, his determination, and his consistency lead to his success? Ditto for Hugh. He loved writing and wrote in every spare hour and observed this:

"Would I have spent every spare hour writing were it not for my dreams? I doubt it. Would I have persisted for three years and eight publications if I confused those dreams for goals? No way. I would have given up after the first or second novel. I allowed myself to dream. I fought for goals that I knew I could attain."

People achieve success and think it's this or that. I did *this* and readers discovered my books. Or I did *that*, and I found an audience. In the end, many of them say luck played a large part because they don't *know* exactly what happened.

They wrote, a lot, they wrote like it was a job (the most glorious job on the planet, but a job) — they "dressed the part". They believed in their stories and their voices. They believed others would like the stories they liked.

FEAR! - Every. F**!#g. Day.

Facing down FEAR every f**!#g day.

Did I read what I wrote in the previous two chapters? Make the mental transition to being a Pro.

This has been infinitely difficult and maybe partially because it's part of the human condition. We're frightened. We like things the way they are. We don't want to lose what we love, and infinitely more important, who we love.

We don't want to lose our reputation or our self-respect. We don't want to face disease or disaster or grief. And we know we will face some of that, and we're deeply afraid, even if we don't recognize it, that we might face far more than we can bear. It's the not-knowing that breeds fear. The anticipation is often worse than the reality.

In the aftermath of the 2018 California Camp Fire, one man whose home burned to the ground said that he was incredibly grateful because his family and pets had survived and they would be okay. Of course, so many people did face the worst in that fire, but I was awed and humbled by his perspective.

Uncertainty breeds fear. The worst-case scenario. The what-ifs when we don't have answers.

Writing is one of the most frightening professions you can undertake...because writing is always uncertain. Even at its best, it never quite matches that Precious Vision that began the process. There are an infinite number of choices in words in character behavior and appearance, in setting, in dialog, in structure, in pacing, in plot.

If you stop to think about all the choices, you could keep writing the same short story for the rest of your life, subtly changing it each day and never run out of variations.

Every time you face the blank screen, the potential for failure is high, perhaps even inevitable because what appears on the screen, the way the story comes together is never what you envisioned. You could have a team of fifteen beta readers and six editors, and still, the story would not be what first appeared in your mind. It would not be perfect. Some readers would love it, and others would hate it.

Writing takes courage and a certain lack of concern for perfection, while requiring the mastery of all the elements of fiction, from imagining characters who come to life, all the way to the mundane use of grammar and punctuation.

Every time I open my laptop, fear lurks in the background. Every time my fingertips touch the keys, fear is hovering just above my hands, willing them to stop moving. I face fear when I start revisions in the morning, when I write a fresh chapter, and when I re-read what I've written at the completion of the first draft.

As a self-published writer, I face fear when I accept a book cover design, when I write a blurb, when I decree a book "finished", and when I click *Publish*. It's fear laced with a thrill of new possibilities, but every f**!#g day, writers face fear.

Don't let it win.

Pearlmaking

Blogs filled with the personal experiences of writers who pursued digital self-publishing early and fervently were the beacons showing me the way to becoming an Indie Author.

Blogs filled with said personal experiences nearly destroyed my voice and my productivity.

As I tried to change my mindset from a fairy godmother publisher I'd dreamed of to lone wolf, I devoured the blogs of established authors and new writers who had chosen the lone wolf path.

Every day I gobbled up new information on the benefits and freedom and opportunity in digital self-publishing. I read about editing, pricing, and marketing. I read about the experiences that drove authors away from their traditional publishers into going it alone. I read about the restrictions on genre forms and publishing frequency and sometimes woefully inappropriate book covers in the traditional publishing world. I read about the bad behavior of literary agents.

I was shown the shining path to the freedom to write what I wanted and to choose a cover that pleased me. I read about the potential to support myself as a fiction writer instead of giving up the bulk of my books' earnings to a multi-national conglomerate.

Joe Konrath, Kristine Kathryn Rusch, and others all educated me on the ins and outs of how traditional publishing worked, the potential that existed in becoming your own publisher, the nuts and bolts of starting and running a book business, the pros and cons of engaging a literary agent. Later I discovered the blogs of Hugh Howey and Russell Blake, Barry Eisler and David Gaughran. I learned about the industry and what other indie authors were thinking by reading The Passive Voice blog and KindleBoards, now called KBoards.

I was a sponge. I read the comments faithfully, sometimes learning more from other writers than I did from the original posts. Joe Konrath's blog sometimes had upwards of one hundred comments that provided sales data and the results of pricing experiments.

These blogs were a lifeline. They helped me, especially Joe and Kris, when I was terrified that I was making a terrible mistake, taking a plunge into the rapids from which there was no turning back. In rough, tough talk, they reminded me that I should spend my time writing, not marketing, despite all the valuable sales and marketing information provided. I loved the virtual kick in the pants that Russell Blake gave — demanding that I ask myself — *Do you want to do this or not?* They offered entertaining, well-substantiated, knock-down experience about their careers and they told me over and over: *Write more. Get better.*

I was inspired by Joe's sharp words — *Why are you reading this? Why aren't you writing?*

They told me about their experiences talking to other writers who struggled to juggle writing careers with day jobs because it was very difficult to make a living in the traditional publishing model.

They debated, they argued, they debunked myths. They boosted my confidence and reassured me. They fired me up and drove me to stick to my writing schedule above all else. They painted graphic pictures of the incredible opportunity to fulfill my fiction writing dreams through self-publishing.

In the comments, I found pointers to formatting ebooks and discussions about genre and marketing. I read debates about pricing and exclusivity versus broad distribution. I found out about the Print On Demand company I use — Lightning Source. I learned about scams and, I admit, wallowed in the furious, raging debates between proponents of indie vs. traditional publishing.

The knowledge I gained from these writers and their generous offering of insight was invaluable, and so I bought their books — both fiction and books on writing and publishing.

But.

I was a woman in the desert — gulping water, splashing it on my face, jumping into the river. I'd hit a speed bump in my novel, I'd feel a prick of doubt (or a sword) when I looked at my meager book sales, and I'd go rushing for a shot of inspiration. I read blogs when I was supposed to be writing. I read blogs when I was supposed to be working at my day job. I read blogs in the middle of the night, and I read them on my phone when I was standing in lines. There was so much conflict over the expanded choices for writers, the tension was not unlike reading a thriller. The advice was useful, the peer support was awesome. I didn't comment much, but when I did, I met new writers.

Most of all, I was reminded every single day that I'd made the right choice and that persistence would win out.

But my addiction to more information, always making sure I knew every single nuance of what I was getting into, interfered with writing. I'd spend entire Saturday afternoons, the one day a week completely devoted to writing fiction, devouring blogs and comments and forum discussions.

As the years passed, the talk of writing to market made me waver. Maybe I should try something different, maybe I needed heroic characters, not the anti-heroes I love. Most of the best sellers were creating enviable or admirable or lovable heroes and heroines. Maybe there wasn't a place in the world for my dark neurotics and sociopaths.

Reading about the market and what was selling began to not only distract me from getting words written, it was subtly freezing my voice. It took me three years to figure this out, and another year or more to take action.

As I write this, I'm on a blog starvation diet. Fortunately for me, some of my go-to trend-setters have stopped blogging. I don't want to be in the dark about the industry, so I try to touch base with The Passive Voice and KBoards from time to time, but never in my writing room. Well, hardly ever.

At the end of the day, all these writers told me to write. Write more books. Focus on what I love — the craft of writing, the act of storytelling. Their words often made me think of one of my favorite comments by Stephen King — "It's the grit of sand that makes the pearl, not attending pearl-making conventions with other oysters."

I finally took their primary advice to heart. I'm a writer. I need to write. I want to write. I finally saw that only writing and improving my skill would get me the career I craved.

I learned enough to feel I passed college courses on self-publishing. Every one of them provided an invaluable service. But most of all, they urged me to focus on the most important thing. Writing.

One word of caution — there is a wealth of information out there in books, blogs, and forums. But there is an ocean of negativity so read with your filters on high. (That's as much a reminder to myself as anything, a reminder I need on a regular basis.)

And if you're an information glutton like I am, and you've never taken a blog or discussion forum or even a social media vacation, I highly recommend it. Try it for a day and see what happens. You might get a lot of fiction written.

Remind Yourself Why

Why did you want to be come a fiction writer?

I wanted to be a fiction writer because I loved reading. I wanted to create those imaginary worlds and give to other people the utterly absorbing pleasure I felt when I was lost in the pages of a novel. I loved the feeling of not being able to put a book down, eager, anxious even, to know what would happen next.

The thought of my words flowing through the minds of others, making them see the world in new ways, eliciting strong feelings, and satisfying their minds and their lives with a meaningful ending was like magic.

Three or five, ten or twenty years in, when your thoughts are drifting constantly toward sales ranks and genre questions, marketing and reviews, and writing schedules, that long-ago desire to write novels gets smothered.

Too often the pleasure has faded while I pushed myself to finish a first draft or torn my hair out over revisions.

Once a writer steps onto the publishing stage, no matter whether it's self- or third-party publishing, there are so many things to think about, the to-do list and marketing considerations have a way of puncturing the creative bubble.

Wondering whether your opening has a strong enough hook and whether the story will fit into a recognizable genre can mess with your head, and worse, it can freeze your fingers on the keyboard and tie your brain into knots.

I love the act of watching my thoughts and ideas escape through my fingertips in long, wonderful ribbons of prose. When I read about writers who dictate their fiction, I can't imagine doing that.

Part of the magic for me is watching how surprising dialog and unexpected interior monolog and twists in the plot appear out of nowhere because your brain is always moving more quickly than your fingers, and this creates a different kind of inroad to the subconscious than speaking does.

I love writing. I love crafting stories. I love describing settings that can become characters in their own right.

For me, my purpose is to express my view of the world, to explore the minds of human beings, to put life and its mysteries into a shape that others can find access to.

Why did you want to become a fiction writer? Write it down, and don't forget. Look at it often. It helps keep you centered and filled with passion.

EDITORS & EDITING

Outing My Editor

The person you're sleeping with can't give you useful and unbiased feedback on your writing. He just can't.

My writing teacher offered this vivid illustration about getting feedback to improve and polish your work. Everyone in the publishing industry agrees. The guy or gal in your bed can't be honest, won't be honest. She doesn't want to hurt your feelings. He doesn't want to piss you off. Writers are too invested, too protective, too connected with their work, making the risk of honesty too great, and so a partner will pull his/her punches when giving feedback on your work.

My husband is a little different. I'm sure my writing teacher would disagree with that statement also. We all think we're "different", but bear with me.

First, he reads fiction — a lot. He read classics for pleasure when he was a teenager. He's read every novel Stephen King, Dean Koontz, Michael Connolly, John Connolly, Lee Child, and Ian Rankin have written, and hundreds more besides. He's read literary fiction and pulp fiction. He's read all of Harry Potter and all of James Bond. And that's just scratching the surface. He's read all of Shakespeare's plays. He reads philosophy, religion, history, and politics. He reads books about grammar and astronomy. He reads biographies and books about Einstein's work. Until we became a digital-news household, he read the two local newspapers and the Sunday New York Times. Now he reads news and opinion and analysis from a host of publications online.

But more importantly, he's brutally honest. And I mean brutally. He's turned my face red on more than one occasion with his casual truth-telling no matter who he's speaking to. And this is why I trust his feedback. He's the rare man who doesn't hesitate to say — *Yes, those pants make your butt look fat.*

My husband is my editor.

He's my first reader, my proof-reader, and my editor.

Outrageous.

Shameful!

Typical self-published writer not caring about editorial quality.

I've chosen him as my editor for three reasons. Not because I can't afford to pay an editor, but because of this —

1. He *gets* the kind of story I want to tell. He doesn't suggest I give my prickly characters puppies to soften them up. He often adds punctuation I don't want, but he leaves my rambling voice alone.

2. He reads widely and voraciously, already noted.

3. This is really the inverse of #1 — I've heard too many stories of traditionally published writers who don't get any true editing, only proofreading and copy edits. And I've seen the results of that "professional" editing in traditionally published books by well-known authors that have typos, consistency errors, and factual errors. Twice in the novel I'm currently reading, I've been jarred out of the story by small mentions of places and phrases that did not exist in the time period in which the novel is set.

I've heard too many horror stories of agents insisting upon re-writes to what they believe will sell, of editors requiring re-writes to their vision of a story. Re-writes that created an entirely different story, that gutted the heart of the book.

Worse, after reading novels with flaccid pacing and other flaws, I've run smack into acknowledgements praising the editor for making the book "so much better" for "making it what it is". Enough said.

Developing a solid working relationship with the editor in my bed has not been easy. It's involved shouting, tears, and stealth changes to the final manuscript. By me, not him.

But twenty novels and twelve novellas in, we have a good process.

I had a lot of hours of self-doubt about my decision to let him edit my books without having another outside eye. We've battled typos and had to re-publish several books. I received one email pointing out my editorial errors citing page number and line. Yet, I disagreed with several of the editorial beliefs expressed in that email, confirming my belief that a certain portion of editing is opinion and taste.

On one level, editing is an art. My editor and I loosely adhere to the ideas expressed in *The Glamour of Grammar* by Roy Peter Clark — readability is more important than blind adherence to "rules", some of which are debated by editors anyway. Striving to write as people truly think and speak is more important to me than grammatical perfection, if there is such a thing.

Most importantly, as I've said to the point of insanity — voice is everything. Voice is what attracts fanatical fans. And that man sleeping beside me does not stifle my voice. Ever.

My books have received reviews that praised the editing, and reviews that criticized it. Sort of like traditionally published books. So I feel confident. Now. For the most part. I didn't always. And honestly, for all my yammering about not needing outside approval and reviews, it was the reviews and fan mail that made me accept that my readers like the way I write, run-on sentences and all.

I finally thanked this patient man who has read all of my books and stories more times than I can count. It took me six years before I acknowledged his contribution in one of my novels. It's taken longer to proudly and indiscriminately tell people that the guy I sleep with edits my fiction for publication. Scary and fun.

It makes for an always-exciting marriage.

Cooking the Books

After self-publishing for eight years, my business partner, editor, roommate and I have developed a process that works. Developing that process was incredibly painful and had a fair amount of finger-pointing involved when we were alerted to typos after a book had been published.

I was hell-bent on having books with the same quality as the best traditionally published book. My husband is more easy-going, and while he's dedicated to quality, he doesn't commit hari-kari when a published book has a typo. He quietly fixes it and republishes the book.

Our current process looks like this:

I write the novel with daily revisions trying to keep the plot relatively hole-free by the end of the first draft. Like all writers, I do a lot of editing myself. After the first draft, I read the manuscript and look for major flaws or missing elements in plot, backstory, and foreshadowing.

He reads it as an ebook and tells me whether the story works, where it dragged, if the character motivations make sense, if he's gripped, if the ending is satisfying. He answers the fifty other questions I shoot at him while he's trying to read.

For many years, he invariably paused to comment on typos and glitches such as this person stood up twice. Invariably, I snapped at him that I could fix the damn typos later, how was the story? After years of this, he's learned to focus on the story.

I go through the book and fix the big issues and complete fact-checking and minor research points.

I edit the book chapter by chapter, adding more depth, cutting repetition, and fleshing out weak scenes.

I use the text-to-voice function to let the computer read the book to me. This uncovers a lot of minor inconsistencies, convoluted sentences, and helps make the dialog crisper.

He prints the manuscript and uses a ruler to edit line by line.

Next, he and I go through his notes as well as my final notes and ~~argue about~~ agree on what needs fixing. These editorial review sessions used to be filled with sharp words and cold shoulders. But I've grown better at taking his feedback. Sort of.

He uses Grammarly to find repeated words, lingering typos, and comma corrections. Often, he disagrees with Grammarly, and since he knows my intent and my style intimately, he's able to ignore where appropriate.

He formats the paperback and orders a proof copy.

He reads the paperback. Reading it like a book surfaces any issues we've missed.

We format the ebook and hit publish.

Sounds simple, doesn't it?

NUTS & BOLTS

Learning Craft

There are hundreds of books on the craft of writing fiction. I've easily read fifty or more, and I have another ten or so that I've started and still sit on my shelves, virtual and physical, with bookmarks reminding me what I still want and need to learn.

Because I bought those books when the elements of the craft were finally starting to take root in my bones, reading those books became less urgent.

The doing of something, once it becomes embedded as instinct, has its own engine driving it. But it's good to feed it with new information — to remind yourself what you've forgotten was important, to learn something that eluded you in the past because it seemed unimportant.

I took classes and studied books on scene-making and character development. I read books about screenwriting to help me learn about structure. If there's an element of fiction that's necessary in a novel, you can be sure I had an entire book on that element.

Sometimes I wonder how much those books really helped me in terms of applying them to my writing. I learned about the topic, I learned the pieces that are needed to build a good story, but reading about how to swing a tennis racket and teaching your body how to move the racket through space are two very different things.

More than all the books I read and underlined and highlighted and starred and re-read, the way I learned craft was by writing. Period.

Years ago I read that James Michener said once you'd written one million words, you would be a competent writer. I set that goal and tracked my word count until I hit that "magic" number. I definitely felt more confident and competent at that point.

Earlier, tongue-in-cheek, I mentioned *Outliers* by Malcolm

Gladwell. More seriously, I took his comments about the need to practice for ten thousand hours to gain a professional level of expertise. Being the spreadsheet-lover that I am, I also began counting my hours.

It might be the placebo effect, but I felt a change in my writing when I passed that milestone. It didn't seem like such a battle to write a novel. I no longer felt I was wrestling an octopus (and the rest of her family) when I made revisions.

Writing, even when it was just typing endless complaints in my journal, is what taught me how to write. Writing hundreds of pieces of flash fiction and fistfuls of short stories helped the concepts of structuring a novel work their way into my bones so that I didn't have to consciously focus on it with every single scene. Using a very short story to learn craft makes learning more manageable. You can see the whole thing at once. It's easier to determine where you went off track.

If you've ever dabbled in flash fiction or thought about it, I highly recommend it. Writing flash fiction is satisfying, first of all, because a story can be written in a single sitting, leaving you feeling very accomplished. Keeping the word count to one thousand words or less challenges your creativity. And there's the learning structure thing. Flash fiction helps you work on crafting engaging first lines because you need to draw the reader in very fast. Flash fiction helps with the removal of excess words as you work toward that rigid word count, re-crafting sentences to tighten them and seeing how using fewer words is often more elegant, observing first-hand how cutting words and phrases makes the writing flow smoothly, sentence to sentence, paragraph to paragraph.

Flash fiction will help you build characters with a single brush stroke, and it will help you think about impactful endings. All of that will feed itself into your longer stories and novels.

I have a box full of short stories I wrote but never did anything with. I have a novel "in a drawer" that's disappeared into the ether. Not all stories work, but they all teach you something new about your style and the act of writing. Every story teaches you how to avoid dead ends in the future and how to keep pacing even.

I'm lazy. I liked learning in the small space provided by short fiction rather than the years that similar lessons might take with novels. This doesn't mean there's not a whole lot more involved in pacing and structuring in a novel, elements that never come up in short fiction. But the shorter work builds your muscles. Working out regularly with shorter runs prepares you for the marathon of a novel.

Reading books, loving them, and wanting to write like the authors I was reading taught me how to write by example. The elements of fiction were absorbed into my cells and stored in my subconscious, and ready to become stronger while I practiced doing it myself.

With all that, learning the craft of fiction is a lifelong pursuit. I'm up for it, are you?

Conflict is Critical

Every day from December 12, 2013, through the beginning of the new year, I grabbed the daily newspaper and looked for an update on Jahi McMath.

Jahi was a thirteen-year-old girl in Oakland, California who was declared brain dead after surgery that her family described as a tonsillectomy. The conflict began when medical professionals insisted there were other factors — they were performing a complicated procedure to improve her breathing along with the removal of her tonsils. You can read more about Jahi here.

Was I ghoulish? Possibly. Reading about her was compelling in part because her story had all the elements of page-turning fiction.

A girl went into the hospital for a tonsillectomy and adenoid removal to correct sleep apnea. She started bleeding. She went into cardiac arrest and was diagnosed as brain dead. Her very religious family refused to believe she was dead, in part because, at times, she seemed responsive to touch.

The elements of compelling fiction were embodied in her story.   1.   Fierce parental love

2.   Injustice (the hospital personnel came across as callous and utterly fixated on avoiding a lawsuit)

3.   The family's unwavering belief in miracles

4.   Medical professionals' determined belief in

scientific truth, accuracy, ethics

   5.   Life and death stakes — reputation and despair, faith and ethics, and most important of all, Jahi's life

Conflict and its importance to fiction can be illustrated by looking at a thousand, a hundred-thousand different novels. I'll talk about Joyce Maynard. Two of her novels were made into critically acclaimed movies, so I'll ignore those — *To Die For* (1995) and *Labor Day* (2013).

I discovered Joyce Maynard through her memoir — *At Home In the World*. I've read most of her novels. I love her writing.

When I read the blurb for her novel, *The Good Daughters*, it sounded intriguing — "A spellbinding novel about friendship, family secrets, and the strange, unexpected twists of fate that shape our lives."

The novel was not spellbinding. Instead, it was one long stream of *telling* about things — about farming, about how the mother behaved, about how the father acted, about crushes on boys, about sexual coming of age, about wanting a child, about feeling left out, about parental failures, about obsessive love. As a reader, I never shared in only one or two of those moments.

I never felt the main character's pain over her mother not loving her. That's because all she did was tell me about her mother's lack of love, complain about how her mother was distant, complain about how her mother seemed to have to force herself to ask her daughter about her day at school. She never revealed those feelings in a scene where I was able to see and touch and taste and *experience* that rejection.

Most of the scenes were moments of happiness — lovers completely joined with each other, the joy of farming (again), and the pleasure of being connected to the land.

Ms. Maynard's subsequent novel, *Under the Influence*, indeed held me spellbound, although unlike *The Good Daughters*, it didn't promise to.

Like all of her work, *Under the Influence* was beautifully written. From the book's beginning, vivid scenes helped me feel the protagonist's grief over the loss of her marriage, her intense love for her son, and her shame and heartbreak over the foolish mistakes that had led to a loss of custody. I was drawn into the unlikely friendship she discovered, feeling the intrigue and appeal of the couple who took her under their wing, seeing their menace before she did, longing for her to find the strength to cut them out of her life.

As her obsession grew, I experienced it right beside her.

Conflict! We hate it in real life, and in fiction it possesses our souls. Intensely readable fiction has conflict at its heart. Compelling characters fighting for their lives, whether physical or psychological or both.

Because we want to eradicate conflict in our real lives, we crave the tension and the promise of resolution it produces in fiction. Resolution is so often denied in the course of our lives — it's one of the reasons our souls demand stories.

Zombies Versus Detectives

It's all about people. Conflict isn't compelling unless readers are drawn into the characters.

Novels, TV shows, and movies have all taught me about character. For some reason that I can't figure out, characters on TV shows make me think about the craft of characterization in a more focused way. Maybe this is because I start analyzing them when I'm watching a series where characters evolve (or don't) over the course of a show's run. Maybe when I'm reading a novel, I'm experiencing it alone, so I'm less prone to discuss. When I'm watching a show, I'm sitting beside my husband, asking him to hit pause so I can pontificate on the characters and their choices.

Two shows that I watched a few years ago around the same timeframe brought characterization into sharp focus for me — the first seasons of *Walking Dead* and *True Detective*.

I was so bored by *Walking Dead*. I never watched it again after the first episode. With *True Detective*, I mourned when that first season featuring Matthew McConaughey and Woody Harrelson came to an end.

At first, it was difficult to figure out what I'd learned from the utter boredom and rage over lost time that I felt with the zombies compared with the addictive desire to gobble up every episode in a festival of binging that I felt after each segment with the detectives.

I thought it might be the zombies themselves. I'm not a zombie aficionado, and I'm very squeamish. But that wasn't really the problem.

The boredom versus addiction was caused by the characters.

In discussing trying to make characters "likable", Alan Watt says — "What makes the heroine heroic is the relentless pursuit of a goal. If she doesn't get what she wants, her life will be unimaginable." Alan goes on to list the primal wants: "love, revenge, lust, justice, loyalty, fidelity, ambition, power, freedom, approval, respect, security, validation, hope, meaning, comfort, answers, fame, wealth, and the desire to conquer." — Alan Watt, *The 90-Day Novel*

In the first episode of *Walking Dead*, season one, the main character's primal want was vague to me. He had a desire for his wife to be happy, but he wasn't doing anything about it. He wanted to find out what the hell happened to bring all these zombies upon the town, but he wasn't trying to find out. He was absorbed with his shock, as anyone would be, but it felt limp to me. Anyone would be shocked if zombies began devouring their neighbors. But I didn't foresee that happening in my neighborhood, and there wasn't enough to make me suspend my disbelief over their sudden appearance.

In *True Detective*, Marty knew without a single doubt there was a certain *way* to be a detective. His partner Rustin was not behaving in that acceptable way. Marty was obsessed with wanting the other man to respect (primal want) the profession that defined him.

Marty also had strong ideas about want he wanted from his wife. And he believed it was a man's right to have a woman on the side for blowing off steam, a right his wife should understand (loyalty, approval, freedom, respect). So as much as I loathed that character's belief system, his well-portrayed primal needs were compelling. I couldn't look away. The character grabbed me even though I didn't like the way he thought or behaved.

Equally strong was Rustin's drive to get inside a killer's head. He wanted answers (primal need), and he was willing to sacrifice his own life to the numbing effect of alcohol to drown the horror of going to such a dark place in his pursuit of a killer.

If you've never analyzed characters in a TV show or movie where they enter your mind larger than life, give it a try.

Focus

"Good writing begins with directing a reader's gaze to something in the world. A writer does not focus on what a character is wearing, but why." — Source Unknown

This quote above lived on my laptop screen for several years. The second line shifted my view of building characters in a very profound way. Simple, really.

It's tedious to read that a woman is wearing black slacks, a black shirt that's a spandex cotton blend covered by chiffon panels, giving a flowing, wraith-like impression. This is topped by a business jacket. Her shoes are black flats with buckles around the ankles, open sides, and come to a sharp point in front. Nothing too interesting there. Tedious. Downright boring. But what if she's wearing flats because she's tall and she's always been self-conscious about her height, and she works in a business environment where easily fifty percent of the men are the same height as her? She doesn't want to draw attention to herself, doesn't want to be overly intimidating, doesn't want her appearance to play into it at all, but wants respect for her intellect and abilities. And the chiffon and cotton blend? She knows she needs to dress for the business world, but her heart is in the arts, so she succumbs to a slice of whimsy in her clothing.

When I began writing this section, I'd titled it *A Writer's Job*. I have no idea why. I wrote a few paragraphs on the writer's job, meandering around entertainment versus exploring the human condition, then veering off to a few brief comments on losing focus from the pleasure of writing fiction because the publishing side of writing can draw you away to a multitude of must-do tasks. I was frustrated and annoyed, feeling I had nothing to say on the subject after all.

During dinner, I whined to my husband that I was struggling with my current novel. I was concerned I should have more backstory on one of the main characters, I was worried I didn't have critique group input advising me to *go deeper* here or there, or, preferably, telling me it was great as it stood. And yet I know with every fiber of my being that critique group feedback can be dangerous, that it can lead to writing a book that is not my own, but a committee book, or someone else's book. It's a very short step to the edge of that treacherous cliff.

I went on about the less prominent character. I rambled more about how I had more detail on the woman's life at this moment in the story timeline, using those details to show her fragile state and almost imperceptible descent into madness.

He said what he always says, write your book, stop over-thinking, etc. Etc. *ETC!*

I ~~wasted time~~ gave myself a brain break by scrolling through the ever-changing newsfeed. Suddenly it slammed into my brain. The quote above and this section are about that very problem — where to go deeper, where to cut, where to focus.

Engaging writing directs a reader's gaze to some *thing* — a character's action or mindset, a disagreement or betrayal, a setting. I'm the writer. I know where I want the reader's gaze to focus.

Every single story can take a hundred different directions, go deeper into one character rather than another, slow down, speed up.

It doesn't matter if I don't go any deeper into this male character. I'm directing the reader's gaze to this woman, to her journey. Yes, my male character is a big part, a key part, but the story is hers. Writing a novel is a camera lens, moving it this way and that until one image comes into sharp focus.

Stephen King said an opening line is crucial — "An opening

line should invite the reader to begin the story. It should say: Listen. Come in here. You want to know about this."

Focus.

A Jury of Peers

"She's the turd in the punchbowl." —Anonymous

Conventional wisdom urges writers to join a critique group. Writers must have multi-faceted feedback on their work. I don't entirely disagree, there are some good things in group feedback, but there are also a lot of pitfalls in critique groups. I managed to plunge into several.

I belonged to a critique group aka writing class for about a year and a half. It appealed to me because it wasn't just a free-for-all. The critique format was well-structured, and the meetings were facilitated by a published fiction writer. Along with the others in the group, she gave us feedback on our work. She also provided weekly in-class writing assignments to stretch us.

The class-slash-critique group wasn't inexpensive, and I thought the hefty price tag would filter out those who weren't serious about writing regularly and improving their work. It did, sort of. But I was still a loner when it came to a burning desire to build a career as a writer. The others loved writing, many were very good writers, and a few were half-heartedly seeking publication.

Three or four members would be "up to bat" each week. With twelve group members, you came to bat once every three weeks or so. The "batters" emailed their short story or a few chapters of their novel by the Friday before class. Each person provided written feedback that was brought to the meeting. The feedback requirements included making check marks where the writing was good, notations where a passage could be improved, and a summary paragraph of feedback on the entire piece.

During class, members read or paraphrased their comments, followed by discussion of the varying reactions to the work. The teacher waited for other members to weigh in before providing her input. The writer at-bat was not allowed to offer any explanation. S/he had to listen silently to all discussion. At the end, two questions were allowed.

The structure was good. It let me know what to expect, it provided positive feedback throughout the work, and the summary comments started with the positive. I liked that we had to focus our thoughts before we started talking. I liked that my submissions had written comments to review later. I'd been in one-day critique groups where writers read their work aloud, but there was no time to digest or think through your thoughts, and the off-the-top-of-your-head comments didn't provide a lot of useful direction.

What didn't work in the class, and this is a problem with nearly all critique groups, was that if you were submitting a novel, it took approximately two years to work through your entire novel. This meant no one was really reading your work as a novel, but in chunks, with several weeks between each handful of chapters. Because the classes ran for four months at a time, there were a few newcomers in each session. Some who had never read your work were critiquing the middle of a novel they knew nothing about. Others who had previously provided useful feedback were no longer there.

For this reason, ninety-five percent of the feedback fell into two categories:

—Comments on the "writing" but not on story-telling, because there was no way to give that kind of input on a novel read piecemeal.

—Feedback that centered around characters at that moment in time — *I don't like her. Why would she do that? I want to know more about her relationship with her father.* After a while, this became incredibly unhelpful. First, because they were questions formed in a partial vacuum, and second, because they became repetitious. When someone had no input, they *wanted to know more* about XYZ. Of course they did, they hadn't read the previous three or six or twelve chapters.

Still, it was social. It was supportive. It involved writers talking about writing. Members brought cheese and wine. When someone had a short story accepted for publication or experienced other writing milestones, the teacher popped open a bottle of champagne to celebrate.

It was fun. We talked books. We received updates on the teacher's progress with her agent and publishing efforts for a new novel, learning a bit about the industry in the process. Positive comments about my writing were affirming. Discovering what didn't work in others' novels or short stories helped teach me what to look for in my own writing. We did learn, we just didn't make a lot of progress toward producing publishable fiction.

There were two absolutely astounding lessons I learned in that class.

The first came when the group was discussing a draft of my first novel — *The Demise of the Soccer Moms*. As the ten women and one man discussed the behavior of my protagonist in the opening scene, one woman gave a friendly laugh. "She's the turd in the punch bowl, isn't she." No question mark, a statement of fact.

Others were horrified. I laughed weakly. Well, yes, she'd had a traumatic experience as a child. She's in the grip of debilitating fear. She's an over-protective mother and an anxious wife. But a turd? The teacher rushed to mitigate the harsh words. All of the guidelines for the group were focused on being supportive and encouraging.

Actually, I wasn't overly upset. It was kind of funny, and it was an excellent lesson in receiving blunt reactions to your writing.

The novel originally had a prologue with a scene portraying a ten-year-old girl witnessing her mother's rape. In a previous class session, I'd been advised to remove the prologue, to use it as backstory. I was told the prologue didn't fit the title of the book (it was about soccer *moms*). The teacher proclaimed that prologues were out of fashion. Plunge into the story.

Maybe. Maybe not. Maybe that rule can't be slapped on every single story that's told. Maybe that prologue was necessary to help readers develop empathy for this woman.

My classmate apologized for being so harsh, but she was a charming woman, and it was difficult to take it in the cutting way the words sounded. Still, the words have stayed with me for over ten years.

A few months later, I put the prologue back where it belonged. I published the book with the prologue it needed, and readers devoured it, punchbowl turd and all.

The second incident occurred on a warm summer evening. Class was conducted at the end of a sloped backyard on a covered patio near the swimming pool. Behind us was a fence covered with sweet-smelling jasmine. We sipped our Chardonnay and enjoyed the warm evening air. This time, I'd submitted a short story. I'd needed a break from the relentless request to *know more about…in* my novel.

The story was very short — only 2500 words.

Flesh it out, was the first suggestion.

Then came the inevitable *I want to know more — about her marriage, about her son, about why this is happening at this moment in her life.*

I was advised there was *too much telling not enough showing*. There were more requests for backstory. Then one woman spoke up rather quietly. "This is a tour de force. You should submit it to Zoetrope Magazine."

Was she saying that about *me*? No one had ever said anything remotely like that about my fiction. It seemed a bit over the top, but after being told my protagonist was a turd, I decided to enjoy it.

Then, amazingly, I re-wrote the story! I added scenes and backstory. I revealed more about the woman's marriage, son, and why this was happening at this point in her life.

My husband read it. "The first version was better."

That was his only feedback.

I looked up the website for Zoetrope Magazine. I saw they held an annual fiction contest. It was the 11th year — *Oh! My lucky number!*

The entries would be judged by Joyce Carol Oates — *Oh! Oh! My favorite author.*

I submitted the story — all 2500 un-fleshed-out words.

When I received the email that out of thousands of entries, Joyce Carol Oates had selected my story and six others for honorable mentions, I cried. For weeks, I cried every time I thought about it. That honorable mention gave me the confidence to keep going. It continued to give me confidence for years.

The lesson? Fiction is taste. Yes, there's strong writing and weak writing. But reactions to a story and even writing styles are very much about personal taste. Agents. Publishers. Instructors. Most important of all, really the only ones who are important at all — Readers.

At the same time I was participating in the critique group, I took a year-long novel-writing class from the same instructor. The class met one Saturday a month and didn't involve critique. Just instruction in the craft of writing a novel and the assignment of a writing buddy to bounce ideas and writing angst off between classes. The idea was to write the first draft of a novel during the length of the course. Also included were two private sessions with the teacher for feedback on partial progress, and a final written and verbal critique of the completed novel.

At my final one-on-one critique, the teacher advised me that my characters were quite unlikable.

She suggested I make my protagonist more appealing by giving her a puppy.

Really? That's how you write fiction? Adding gimmicks like puppies? Force-fitting devices onto a character into whom you hope to breathe life?

Maybe I should make her a tennis player, or an excellent baker of luscious chocolate desserts. Except that was not the character who had come to me. That wasn't the story I was telling.

But the voice of publishing expertise lingered and eventually I decided I would follow it, with a twist.

My character was a woman who was relentlessly and aggressively working to ascend the corporate ladder. Every morning before dawn, she ran several miles. She worked long hours. She lived in a sleek, minimalist condo in Palo Alto, California. She didn't have time to take walks with a puppy! So, I gave her an elegant, elaborate, spiky, fierce-looking, venomous Lion Fish that she cared for very much. My character empathized with this fierce creature. Maybe some writers' characters have puppies. In general, mine don't. Mostly because I love puppies and I don't know if my characters would be the most devoted pet owners.

That said, I learned a lot from my critique group and the classes I've taken. This is just a cautionary tale about being alert to the dark side and receiving feedback with a discerning ear.

Lessons From Breaking Bad

Winner of two Golden Globes and countless Primetime Emmy awards, the critically acclaimed TV show, *Breaking Bad*, was released in 2008.

I watched the first episode sometime in the 2008-2009 timeframe. I didn't like it. I thought it was boring, if I recall correctly. People kept urging me to watch it, and I kept dismissing them — *Tried it, didn't like it.*

Finally, in 2016 or so, we hit a dry spot in finding shows we enjoyed and tried it again. I have no idea what was going on in my head that first time, but this time, I was hooked. I grieved when the series ended. It was literary and gripping, emotionally moving and filled with suspense. The characters were absolutely mesmerizing.

If you've never seen it, put down this book and binge-watch. Seriously. You'll learn more about creating compelling characters than you can imagine.

A short time later I saw a panel discussion with the creator and several writers of the series.

The things they said about the process of developing and writing that award-winning show were a lesson in attitude, hitting squarely at some of my ongoing struggles.

1. Vince Gilligan, the creator, spends very little time on the internet.

I'm in awe of this. I think it adds a certain depth to a writer to tame that always available brain-sucking monster. Writers are ~~required~~ encouraged to be on social media interacting with readers and other writers. We use the internet for research, there's no getting around that. Over the past few years, I've gone from reading a newspaper to getting all my news online. It's always there, always beckoning, always offering a hit of adrenaline to my hungry, effervescent brain.

When I heard Vince talk about how the internet interfered with creativity, I vowed to put a more secure gate around my time spent there.

2. When a TV show is being written, seven writers are in a room tossing around ideas. You can't compare writing a novel with writing a TV show.

This grabbed one of my critical monsters by its tongue. There are quite a few serialized shows that I've loved, that I've been downright addicted to. Shows that made me ache when they came to an end — *Six Feet Under, Breaking Bad, House of Cards, The Killing*, the first season of *True Detective*. I could go on, but I'll stop there.

These shows have such incredible characters I came to feel like I knew them inside and out. Of course, that happens with a lot of fiction, but it's different when you have characters' visual presence. The visual aspect of movies and TV dig deeper into my brain and stay longer. The plots can be incredibly complex and full of multiple twists.

I felt that I couldn't measure up to the entertainment and pleasure they brought me. This reminder of the realities of writing fiction versus writing for the screen helped me change my standards. Slightly.

3. When you're stalled, ask where the character's head is at in this moment in time.

This has been incredibly helpful for a non-plotter like me. It also makes for a story more weighted toward character than plot. With deeper insight into the characters, a plot can unfold in more interesting ways.

4. You can't make a character likable *by giving her a puppy.*
To be honest, I wrote that statement in my notes while listening to the discussion. I can no longer find the discussion... so I don't know if they specifically referred to a puppy or I embellished based on my own hot button, but the point was made. You can't change a character by force-fitting attributes or a certain kind of lifestyle. And why would you want to?

Evolution

After writing novels for going on twenty years, I've developed a solid writing process that works well, feels comfortable, and is mostly fun and satisfying. Those hair-pulling moments are less frequent, and the lost hair is no longer in fistfuls.

In the beginning (that sounds Biblical, but it's anything but), I wrote reams of character notes. When I first started trying to write a novel, I used lists of traits, likes and dislikes, to form characters. I made notes about life events, sometimes creating a yearly timeline for every year of life leading up to the story opening.

When I discovered *The 90-day Novel*, I began using the deeper, more open-ended questions outlined in that book. If you're struggling to build characters or want to achieve more character depth, I highly recommend it. The book directs you to ask your characters questions and record the answers. This technique is common, but the questions in this book are more thought-provoking than most others I've seen. They probe fluid aspects of a character's nature and life experience. The questions and commentary in this book prompted me to think in new ways about the essence of each character.

Working through these questions left me with a one-inch binder containing fifteen-twenty pages of notes for each main character.

Questions for your characters include: *What was the worst day of your life? What will your epitaph say? What do you wish it would say?*

These questions teased out well-rounded characters. But once I began the first draft of the novel, I found myself caught up in telling the story, forgetting to go back and check my characters' biographies. When I got off course from where my notes suggested the character arc was headed, or left out something critical in a character's mindset, I became extremely frustrated. Trying to force-fit a forgotten facet of a character into a story rarely worked.

I hoped the questions had worked themselves into my subconscious, and that anything "missing" might have been deemed unnecessary or irrelevant by my subconscious storyteller. I hoped.

When I started my ghost story novella series, I decided to write in first person, a point of view I'd used only in flash fiction. With a first-person voice, it didn't seem as important to have background notes because I was so intimately inside of that character's head, I figured she would reveal herself as I wrote. And she did.

Eventually, I wound myself around to a place where I let go of my Q&A prep and the results binders of notes for my novels. For me, the notes and background worked brilliantly for several years, but after writing eleven novellas, they began to feel limiting. I didn't like answering questions about childhood experiences or trauma in their lives before their stories had begun to take shape.

Possibly this was just the evolution of my ability to tell a story. Writing more, telling more stories, had developed better instincts.

Writing with only a vague sense of who a character is feels like real life — meeting someone new and gradually getting to know what she's like, then discovering what he cares about, and finally, learning her secrets.

I write without an outline. The closest I ever came to outlining was when I was using the framework from *The 90-Day Novel*. The book also has a detailed structure for the story arc, and when I worked on those exercises, a plot began to emerge before I typed the first sentence.

After several years writing flash fiction, I wanted to write with even less idea as to where I was headed. I liked the experience of being surprised by the story. I loved it when something emerged later in the book that tied to something I'd written earlier, having no idea the pieces would connect.

That excitement of watching my subconscious make connections is beyond thrilling. It's one of the reasons I love to write.

I finally cut loose the character notes once and for all when I wrote my *Haunted Ship Trilogy*. I went for long walks and thought about the story, jotting down ideas on my phone.

The process I've used for about nearly three years and thirteen novels now is this:

I start thinking about a character and how the story might open. Once I have a few ideas for the first chapter. Often, an opening line will come to me when I'm mid-way through writing a different novel.

I start the first draft, writing between 1,000 and 3,000 words a day, taking it easy on Sundays and setting a lower word count goal one other day a week to allow for life activities.

When I first get up, I read and lightly edit what I wrote the previous day. I record what happened in each chapter. Not recording what happened is the biggest issue when I go to revise. Knowing how the story is going is critical, and if I don't make notes on each chapter, I forget. A lot. At the end of my early morning revision session, I jot down questions about the story then go for a long walk. More often than not, I'm flooded with ideas for what's coming next.

For a while, bad weather and a missed walk sent me into a tailspin of unfocused writing. Now, when the weather's bad, I practice the habit of *just write the next line and the next and the next*. I ask the question mentioned by the writers from *Breaking Bad — Where is the character's head at this moment in time?*

Lots of writers love working from an outline. They find the same magic happens as they develop a plot and they also experience the thrill of surprises in the writing.

But this is what works for me, and it makes me love the act of writing every single day because it feels like I'm reading a book that has yet to be written.

The King

I said it earlier, and I'll say it again because it's so important…

"Good writing begins with directing a reader's gaze to something in the world." I never found the source, but it might be Stephen King. He's said enough brilliant things about the craft and the art of writing that it's entirely possible he said this also.

It doesn't really matter. I love the simplicity of this. I love the open-ended quality. It sounds easy, doesn't it?

I like the quote because this is how it all begins. Something in the world that we want to show to other people. We see something — a human trait, a life-changing event, great love, intense hatred, and all the emotions and experiences and unanswerable questions of life. We want, we need to tell other people. (Jerry Cleaver's book, *Immediate Fiction*, talks about this pressing need to tell stories inherent in all human beings.)

We write fiction because we see something and we're compelled to tell others.

In each novel or short story I write, there's something I want to show the world. And often, I don't know my own thoughts about something I've witnessed or experienced until I start to shape them into a story.

This is why I'm drawn to writing a novel without knowing where my story is going. There are a lot of strong opinions on this topic of plotting versus not.

Stephen King helped me understand my own inclination. Whether you like his writing or not, his stories have connected with millions of people. He's invited them inside his mind where they are more than happy to spend quite a few hours. For that reason alone, I respect him, and for that reason, I listen carefully to what he says. (I've only read two of his novels, but I absolutely loved them — *Misery* and *Dolores Claiborne*. I would put *Dolores Claiborne* up against a lot of literary fiction.)

In an interview originally conducted for Writer's Digest in 1991, he had this to say about the process of writing.

C.S. Forrester, the British writer, once described his story-developing process as dropping assorted objects into the water of his subconscious and letting them sit there for weeks or months or years. Eventually, he said, he would feel them merge and meld and take some sort of shape until an idea surfaced and he could start writing. How does that process work for you?

Stephen responded:

Yeah, that's the way it works...The best work that I've ever done has always had a feeling of having been excavated, of already being there. I don't feel like a novelist or a creative writer as much as I feel like an archaeologist who is digging things up and being very careful and brushing them off and looking at the carvings on them.

I don't work from an outline or anything like that.

The thing is, for me, I never get all that stuff out unbroken. The trick and the game and the fun of it is to see how much of it you can get. Usually, you can get quite a lot.

But I love it. I mean, when the stuff just shows up at the right time. You can say to yourself, "Well, I know what's gonna happen for the next 30 pages, but after that, I'm fucked. I don't know." Then it's like a door opens and somebody ambles in and says: "You called for me." And I say: "I don't remember it, but come on in and help me 'cause this is where you're supposed to be. You fit right in here today. Thank you for coming." And that's it.

And they pay you for that.

Despite all my fits and starts with trying to make a living at this, I remember a blog comment early in my self-publishing journey in which a writer said he marveled at every dollar he earned. Even if he only sold one book a month, someone was drawn to his book and paid their hard-earned money to read it.

That's the miracle and the thrill and the driving force of self-publishing. You can put your work out there, and through a lot of blood, sweat, and tears, readers will find it and pay to read what you've written. It takes your breath away.

I'll end with another quote.

"Writing is like driving at night in the fog. You can only see as far as your headlights, but you can make the whole trip that way." — E. L. Doctorow

OPPORTUNITY

This is it!

This is it! (Or not.)

In May 2013, out of nowhere, as these things often are, I received email from an editor at the now-defunct RT Book Reviews — a prominent industry publications read by many bookstore owners.

RT Book Reviews magazine (formerly Romantic Times) is doing a trend piece about suburban noir/domestic suspense in our August issue, and we'd like to include you in the feature.

Do you have some time to discuss suburban noir w/me? I confess I found you thru Google search! And your comments resonated with me so much, I knew we had to get you on board to talk about this.

First...Google search! It works!! An interview?! People have noticed suburban noir? *Industry* people?

Imagine my thoughts: This is *IT*!!! The genre I adopted out of the ether that is really no genre at all is a thing. I'll be interviewed alongside heavy-hitter fiction writers! This article will come out, and readers will flock to my books. *Flock!*

I could hardly breathe. I was beyond excited. I was scared to death. I'm not the most articulate person on the planet. At the time, I'd done a handful of interviews — written interviews. Bloggers sent questions via email, and I had days, weeks to revise and edit and tweak and revise again so I didn't sound like a drooling idiot.

The writer and I scheduled a time for my phone interview.

It was incredible. Somehow, my brain connected with my tongue. Maybe, because I was talking about something I loved (not technology, for example). She asked questions, and I answered and suggested additional angles. She was thrilled by my insights. I was shocked that I had *insights*. We had a conversation instead of a constrained Q&A. I was conversing with a magazine writer! She thought I had something to say. She gave me new things to consider.

When I hung up the phone an hour later, I felt like a real writer.

When the article was published, my whole body was buzzing with anticipation. Sure, she left out what I thought were a few of my better comments, but the translation from my brain to my tongue to her ears and notes, then to her keyboard was smooth and nearly unbroken. I didn't sound like a blithering moron. The cover of my first novel — *The Demise of the Soccer Moms* — was featured alongside Gillian Flynn's *Gone Girl*, Megan Abbott's *Dare Me*, Laura Lippman's *I'd Know You Anywhere*, and Sarah Weinman's *Troubled Daughters, Twisted Wives*.

I had some intermittent, panic-stricken moments that readers would buy my books and scream — this is **nothing** like *Gone Girl*. This was in the wake of *Gone Girl's* runaway success where everyone (aren't they still?) was trying to write the "next" *Gone Girl*. I tried to shut that thought out of my mind.

This was my moment! My books were going to *fly* off the shelves. When the article was published, I was poised to release my fourth novel. The writer had asked about that book but hadn't mentioned it in the article. When she sent the link to the article, she told me she'd look for a way to feature me and again in the future, promoting my latest work.

There I sat, two years later. The article was no longer online, destroying one of my best marketing links. My books did not fly off the shelves. They scarcely trickled. Although suburban noir still pops up in the news, it hasn't drawn attention to my books. I get hits on my website from people searching the term, but so far, they've never turned into clicks to my ebooks.

Then, it happened again in a less dramatic fashion. *The Girl on the Train* hit the top of the New York Times bestseller list and was dubbed suburban noir.

"Google!" I cried, "Where are you? Bring the readers to my books." They continued to come, in the same fits and starts, stopping by to read, nothing more.

What does all this mean? It means striving to make a living as a fiction writer is a roller coaster that can rip your stomach right out of your body.

You Talkin' About Me?

Word of mouth is what sells books.

Everyone knows this.

Random House knows this. Simon and Schuster knows this. Agents know, book editors know, writers know. They will all tell you this in no uncertain terms.

And the psyche-shattering truth of this fact? You can't do a damn thing to make it happen, beyond writing the best books you can and trying to expose them to readers in a way that works for you.

Random House can't make word of mouth happen, and no writer can make it happen. Random House can take out a full page ad in the New York Times. The ad might move a lot of readers to buy the book, but it won't endear the novel to millions of readers. Only the story does that. A writer can Tweet her brains out and attract lots of followers with her witty observations, but it won't make people love the novels she writes.

It's all about the book connecting with lots of readers.

What, really, is word of mouth?

In our imaginations we see people sipping coffee or watching a ball game, asking their friends — *Have you read this book? I couldn't put it down. The story moved me. I was blown away. You have to read it.*

I've been on the giving and receiving end of those statements.

There are books I read five or seven years ago that I still recommend, given the slightest chance to shove my praise into a conversation.

It's frustrating for a writer to know that some nebulous, unseen network holds the future of their books in its collective hands. Outside of our hearing, beyond our awareness, at a time we can't ever know, readers might be talking about our books.

Since Amazon became the behemoth it is, swallowing GoodReads whole, some of this word of mouth takes place in reviews, in comments on reviews, in lists of other books that tell book browsers — hey, other people who bought this book also bought this other book. The silent word of mouth being — *Check it out, you might like it.*

There are scores of advice books, blogs, and workshops telling you how to build a career. Have a business plan. Have a marketing plan. Advertise. This is how to advertise effectively. How to utilize social media to connect with potential readers. Event the blatant but misleading — How to build word of mouth!

I could fill the rest of this book with lists of teasing emails I've received, ads that have tracked me relentlessly, and books that promise my effectiveness will skyrocket.

I agree with all of those things. I have a business plan. I regularly update my marketing plan. Sometimes, the marketing plan changes daily. I've taken webinars and joined groups to discuss how to effectively advertise fiction.

But all of this is simply letting potential readers know that your books exist at all. Word of mouth can't be written into a plan.

In *The Tipping Point*, Malcolm Gladwell says a product or trend needs three things to take hold — the law of the few, the stickiness factor, and context. If you haven't read the book, I recommend it. You can also find the basic concepts on Wikipedia.

The law of the few refers to people with certain skillsets who excel at passing along information, connecting with others, and selling. In other words — Word. Of. Mouth.

You can't buy word of mouth. You can't truly study it. You can't change it. All you can do is sit back and try to enjoy the ride.

More, More, More!

When I read stories of other indie writers, all the successful ones seem to be, claim to be, working harder than me. All the *almost* successful ones are regaling me with tales of how hard those at the top of the bestseller lists are working.

Much harder than I, back-breaking and mind-numbing effort and finger-breaking effort — fourteen hours a day of solid work writing and marketing.

Until recently I rarely paused to analyze this. Fourteen hours a day means working without a break from six in the morning until eight at night. Maybe they were. Maybe they still are.

But the rare times when I did pause to think this through instead of using it to beat myself up, repeating the mindless mantra that success was eluding me because I didn't work hard enough, because I couldn't muster the energy to work after dinner, I remembered my days working in high tech.

My peers moaned with rueful smiles about their fourteen-hour days. These people were not avatars on the internet, they worked in the office across the hall and two doors down and one hallway over from where I sat. I knew they were responding to emails and working on PowerPoint slides at night. I saw their names shimmering in my in-box with post-midnight timestamps when I woke in the morning.

But I also knew that these same people lingered over lunch, telling lengthy stories about their trips overseas. I knew how often they stood in the hallway and complained, sometimes for an hour or more, and I saw through their glass-paneled doors when they gathered a few close friends into their offices for a private gossip and complaint session. I knew how many minutes of a two-hour meeting was spent waiting for people who were late, echoing ideas using different words to be sure everyone made their presence and their "contribution" stand out, listening to long-winded explanations of something everyone already knew, and on and on it went.

One of my all-time favorite Dilbert cartoons depicts Wally asking Dilbert — "What's the lowest ratio of work-to-gabbing that's still considered 'work'?"

Dilbert responds, "I'd have to say one-in-eight, maybe one-in-nine."

Wally says, "Sounds right."

Dilbert replies, "Does talking about work count as work?"

And Wally closes the interaction with, "Well...I'm not enjoying it."

What we label "work" changes from person to person. For my colleagues, it meant physical presence in the office, talking about work, plus work at night and on weekends. I came to believe that many people worked nights and weekends because they chatted and complained all day long. They spent time in the previously-mentioned meetings which were always scheduled to last an hour, and frequently two hours or more. The business accomplished during those one-hour meetings could have been completed in twenty minutes. So I'd say the lowest work-to-gabbing ratio was one-in-three.

I thought of this ratio often as I ate lunch at my desk, using the extra thirty minutes to write. When I avoided gossip sessions and got my work done during the day.

All that said, successful indie writers work hard. Many of them publish several more books a year than I do. They're active on social media, chatting with readers, and in forums, helping new writers, and writing books to share their expertise.

Over the years I wailed regularly that I wasn't doing enough. "Everyone" said I must market regularly, effectively, relentlessly, but what did that mean? How could I have worked in high-tech product marketing for all those years and not have a grasp of what marketing meant? I suppose I did, but I couldn't always translate that knowledge to marketing fiction.

For years, those writers blogged and podcast about their paths to success. Every single one of them talked about marketing, although most admitted…

Tweeting doesn't sell books. True.

Readers in different genres respond differently to different marketing styles. True.

If anyone knew what worked for marketing, including the Big Five Publishers, all books would be successful. All true.

Every single successful indie author talks about one critical ingredient — *Write more books.*

I resisted this for years. In part, because my day job didn't allow time for writing and revising more than two books a year. If I'm honest, part of this was due to my affection for wasting time. And another part was due to still being on a learning curve in finding a process that works for me and simply learning how to construct a novel without seven or eight revision cycles.

Still, I worried I needed to do more. Occasionally, I still do. I complained that I already had a lot of books. I whined and worried that successful writers said they saw sales traction at three books. A year later, they were saying sales will become steady with five published books. Shortly after this came a comment about a writer still looking for her audience and writing her fifteenth book.

The landscape is always changing. When the three-book meme was floated, I only had one published novel. By the time I got to three, conventional wisdom said five. I also ignored the fact that most of the successful writers saying this were writing a series.

Finally, five years into my self-publishing venture, I started writing a series.

Part of my resistance had come from the fact that I couldn't see myself being interested in writing about a cop or an FBI agent for even a single novel, much less ten or twenty. Although

I love TV shows that are extended series, I don't read a lot of series novels.

The only reason I did eventually follow this path was because the series evolved by accident. More about how this happened will be covered later in the book.

When I did start the series, I returned to my weekly complaints about the three-book, five-book magic number and my failure to see the steady success that others experienced.

However, at those milestones, I did start to find an audience. By book five, I'd received quite a bit of fan mail, and reviews were (finally!!) starting to appear below my books. Good reviews. Bad reviews.

I continued my periodic (spelled twice monthly) moaning that I should be *working harder*. Maybe I should put more effort into building a brand on Twitter. Maybe I should increase sign-ups to my mailing list by using the marketing techniques I read about. Maybe I should do this. Or that. Or the other. Maybe I should figure out how I could crank out 5000 words a day like others did.

One day, in the midst of finishing up book six in my series, I suddenly realized I was devaluing my writing. I was acting and talking as if the story was peripheral and all that mattered was quantity and marketing and sales.

After all those years, I now had several hundred fans. I needed to be giving them what they asked for — more books. I didn't need to be tweeting and hosting Facebook groups (if that sort of thing even worked for my genre). I needed to be doing the job I loved. I needed to realize the value of writing more books, improving my craft with every one, but not in a frenzy of production. My readers were happy when I focused on keeping myself in the satisfying realm of flow.

How ironic. When the writer is happy, so are readers!

At the same time, I resisted the *write more books faster* idea because I was so steeped in the model dictated by the traditional publishing industry. One book a year. Maybe one book every two years. Writing faster means you're a hack and I certainly didn't want that. This mindset died hard.

But if I was a writer who focuses on actually writing during her writing hours, who learns how to create an atmosphere of flow, I could write more books than I was. I would write more books because it would be natural. Instead, I was complaining and reading about marketing techniques. [For more about flow, read *Fearless Writing* listed in the recommended reading section.]

I needed to value the actual writing. Readers were sending me email and signing up for my mailing list and writing reviews asking for more books because they liked what I wrote. If I put all that time spent perusing the internet for secrets, trying to be witty on Twitter and friendly on Facebook, I *would* be writing more books. And that's how this whole thing started — I love writing, I love telling stories, I love discovering and watching characters live their lives.

More books do matter. When readers fall in love with your voice, they want more. You can't ever write fast enough to satisfy their desire. I would spend two and a half months writing and polishing a book. A reader would devour it in two and a half days, sometimes less, and ask when the next one was coming.

Traditionally published writers like Joyce Carol Oates, Stephen King, and Nora Roberts have written a lot of books. More than the norm. And the vast majority of successful indies have also written a lot of books. The single or sophomore breakout is an anomaly.

Writing more books does matter, but it also matters that we do it in our style, at our pace. There's working hard, there's wasting time, and there's becoming your own personal sweatshop.

Learn about flow. Read *Fearless Writing*. Seriously.

TIME WAITS FOR NO ONE

W.W.S.K.D.

What Would Stephen King Do? W.W.S.K.D?

If there's a writer who has followed his own vision and built a global following of people who love his writing, it's Stephen King.

He's true to his voice, and he follows his creative instinct seemingly without question. He boldly stated, "I was built with a love of the night and the unquiet coffin. If you disapprove, I can only shrug my shoulders. It's what I have."

I have tried to settle into accepting the fact that I was given an obsession with the human psyche and the darkness inside the mind. I was given the suburbs. Stephen King was once asked why he writes what he does, and he asked, "What makes you think I have a choice?" Settling into the characters that provoke you and the stories you can't stop thinking and dreaming about instead of what sells, is difficult but freeing. Writing what grips you is what makes writing pleasurable.

What were you given?

Hosts of writers have devoured his book — *On Writing.*

It's brimming with encouragement, pointed advice, and an obvious love of fiction.

"Talent renders the whole idea of rehearsal meaningless; when you find something at which you are talented, you do it (whatever it is) until your fingers bleed or your eyes are ready to fall out of your head. Even when no one is listening (or reading, or watching), every outing is a bravura performance, because you as the creator are happy. Perhaps even ecstatic. That goes for reading and writing as well as for playing a musical instrument, hitting a baseball, or running the four-forty."

He goes on to recommend that anyone who wants to be a writer should be reading and writing fiction four to six hours a day. He insists that if you love fiction, this won't seem like a lot, and truly, it's not.

Some of us have highly demanding jobs. Jobs that require travel make it especially difficult to find regular writing time. Some people are caring for several small children or elderly parents or disabled adult children.

But always there is some sort of leisure time, and it all comes down to what we choose to do in those moments or hours. I read that when John Grisham first started writing fiction, he wrote from midnight until two in the morning. He slept for a few hours and then went off to work to practice law, a job that often does demand twelve to fourteen hours a day, or so I've heard.

The majority of fiction writers come to it because they loved the magic of disappearing into the world of a novel when they were younger. We've loved reading fiction all our lives and cannot imagine a life without it.

Being that I have some obsessive-compulsive tendencies, I took Stephen King's guidance and turned it into a rule. I fired up a tab in my spreadsheet and titled it *4-6 hours*. For years, I tracked how many hours I wrote. (Not the hours I sat in my writing chair and complained in my journal or read blogs or vegged out on Facebook and dipped my toes into the river of Twitter, but the hours I wrote and revised fiction.)

I even tracked the hours I read fiction. (Eye roll.) I color-coded the total for every day in a shade of blue I'm fond of. If my day job intervened, when I had a day devoted to family or friends, I colored it light blue, giving myself a pass to actually live my own life instead of the lives of my characters.

On the days I missed my target, I colored the cell dark gray.

Each time I looked at that spreadsheet, I saw all the days I'd focused on what I wanted to do and all the hours that I'd allowed myself to get distracted and discouraged. After a few years, I finally put it aside and looked at my growing shelves of books — the novels I'd written and the novels I'd read and cataloged on GoodReads.

Writers write.

Fiction writers write fiction.

And when you're writing fiction, you aren't thinking about

marketing and book sales and a hundred other things. Time is suspended. You're lost in the lives of the people you've created. And that is pure, endless pleasure. I have no idea why it's so extremely difficult to remember and grab onto that feeling every damn time I sit down in my writing chair.

Stealing Time

I'm lucky to be married to a man who agreed years ago to my idea that we would get up at four o'clock in the morning so I could write fiction for two hours before getting ready for my day job. Yes, this meant we were nodding off by 8:15 pm, but I'm a morning person anyway. And when I sat down to write, when I turned off the internet the minute I went into the writing room, I accomplished a lot in those early hours.

The world was silent, the street outside my window was dark.

Even better, when I headed off to that soul-sucking day job, I felt like I'd done the thing I want to do more than anything else *before* the world poked its head in the door and started demanding I pay attention to other things.

If I was aiming at those four hours recommended by Stephen King, I needed to find time. Writing after dinner yielded varying degrees of success. It's possible. I've done it. I've even produced decent short fiction writing an hour before my head hit the pillow. But by that time of the day my critical voice is more likely to be full of energy and opinions. I'm tired. I was often grouchy over some political antic or stupidity from the day job.

So I stole time. Yes, I stole from my employer.

I found that taking a break to play a game on my phone took three or four minutes. In those three minutes, I could write fifty words.

One of the things I learned in my critique group/writing class came from the exercises the teacher handed us each week. I discovered that writing on demand, without time to analyze, without pressure to be "good", often yielded better writing. It was more interesting and thoughtful and unique. I truly believe that writing with a bit of pressure to simply get words down makes a closer connection to the sub-conscious and we produce stories we didn't even know were lurking back there behind the curtain.

Checking social media or reading blogs about the publishing industry, surfing the web like all high-tech workers, took three to five minutes, often ten. Composing a comment on a blog post took longer. In those three, five, ten minutes, I could write another thirty or fifty words or more.

Conference calls never started on time. Never. And then there was the throat clearing once they did start...

Who just joined? Jane.
Who just joined? Alan.
Who just joined? Greg.
How about that weather?
I can't get the collaboration software to work.
Did everyone get the slides I emailed?
We'll give everyone else another few minutes to join and get going at five after the hour.

If I muted my phone, lowered the volume...

How long are the commercial breaks during a football game? How long does it take to wait for the dentist? How long do you sit in your car waiting for the school bell to ring? How often is the plane delayed? How long do you sit on the runway?

How long do things take, really?

There are small pieces of time scattered throughout most of our days. With a little brain training, you can shift your focus quickly and write a paragraph here or there. Soon, you'll have a chapter and then...a novel.

After all, writers write. It doesn't take much, but at the same time, it takes everything.

Untethering

I know I've mentioned this several times, many times, to the point of madness, but I know I'm not alone in this — my obsessive need to check in with the world. And it's a struggle every hour of every single day.

Several years ago during chit-chat at a work dinner, a co-worker told the group that his wife had gotten angry at him a few weeks prior. She woke at two o'clock in the morning, and he wasn't beside her in bed. She went downstairs to look for him and found him in their home office, checking and answering email.

One out of three Americans check Facebook in the bathroom, according to an AIS Media study in 2011. I imagine it's the same for Twitter. I expect that percentage has grown since 2011.

Digital information has an addictive quality. Our brains like the little candy treat of something new. A new piece of information, a new joke, a new list for self-improvement, a new story, a new scandal, a new connection from a friend, new information on health or science. New, new, new, new.

When I was bored or overwhelmed or at a standstill on a project at work, any time I felt the need for a break, instead of writing (!), instead of getting up and stretching or taking a short walk, which actually would have been beneficial, I checked something. Twitter. Facebook. Blogs. The news feed. Email. It's estimated social media costs the US economy $650B a year in lost

productivity. But corporate America started it! With their emails!!
What does it cost writers?

Employees in my former company were emailing around the clock. Except for Friday evening until Saturday afternoon, somewhere in the world it was between the hours of eight and six. Because I went to sleep early in order to get up before the sun to write, I had a constant low-level buzz of anxiety that I'd miss a request from management popping in at nine o'clock at night. Executive management expected immediate answers. *You all have smartphones, there's no excuse for missing an email. Ever.*

So I checked when I woke. At four a.m. Ninety percent of the time, there was nothing that required a response, and ninety-seven percent of the time, there was nothing demanding an immediate response.

But there was the three percent. And that was enough. Like Pavlov's dogs, I checked. Every day. Sometimes, interrupting my writing to check again at five a.m.

Every weekday morning I had an hour and a half, sometimes two, of gloriously uninterrupted writing time. Yet, over the years I consistently, relentlessly interrupted that valuable time myself — no one else. Between those worrisome work emails, blogs, social media, KBoards, personal email, there is always, always something new to check out.

Day in and day out I slashed through that bubble of quiet fiction writing with a bloodied knife dripping memes, cute animals, screw-ups, action items, and political squabbling. There was absolutely nothing I needed to know about my day job at four o'clock in the morning. But the not-knowing gnawed at me. What if I was blind-sided two hours later? What if I should have used my writing time to work on the project the boss required later that day? What if, what if, what if?

The only way to quit is cold turkey. Like any addiction, the only way out is with the use of drastic measures. I've taken those measures over and over — leaving my phone in another room, turning off the internet. I do well for a day or two, a week or so, and then the addiction takes control once more.

But I don't stop trying because I know that lack of self-discipline destroys my productivity, and worse, interferes with the creative process.

I'm starting again this week — no excuses.

What's your excuse?

Advice From On High

"Would my time be better spent writing?"

That is so what I want to hear. Write to your heart's content. Don't over-rotate to an obsession with marketing. And to some extent, it's true. In a blog post from 2014, that question was addressed.

"So, here's the question: why are so many people squawking at us about our platforms if the numbers are so bad?"

[Oh, yes, those pesky platforms again. Must get me one of those. Maybe tomorrow. Maybe I can find one on eBay.]

"To get some industry insight, I reached out to an author who has published extensively with Amazon Publishing (four books, two different imprints). I chose her because Amazon knows. It doesn't matter what you think of Amazon's role in the publishing industry. Their true business is numbers; that's what drives their success. The advice they gave to my author friend: write more. Don't waste time on social media. **The single biggest factor in whether or not you sell books is whether or not you write books.**"

— Source: CreativeNonFiction.org

Would I be better off writing?

Not exclusively, but to a large extent, yes. This doesn't mean marketing is unnecessary. It means, writing should always come first. It means the quality of your books will do more for you than any platform. Several of my virtual mentors echo this sentiment. It means the desire that got us all into the dream of getting our work into the hands of readers should continue to be the central focus of our dream. Some of the writers who paved the way for me have wholeheartedly agreed:

Hugh Howey: *Never prioritize marketing over your next book. Most marketing tactics don't work.*

Joe Konrath: *Tend your own garden, write more books.*

Russell Blake: *Would that it were so easy.* (Regarding the suggestion that marketing techniques that worked for one writer or genre will translate into success for other writers and genres)

I want to be clear. Marketing is required. The entire next section is devoted to my marketing experiences and the place where I've ended up.

Most writers hate it. All writers are required to do it in one form or another. All. And there's comfort in that. We're all in this together. We're not competing. We might be competing for attention but not for readers. Even if you can write a novel in a single month, readers will finish it before you've written the third chapter in your next book. Readers don't just like a single author. And all of them have favorites, and all have writers they don't care for.

It's not a competition.

MARKETING

An Unstable Platform

You must have a platform!

Who are the members of your tribe?!

Profile your tribe and find out where they hang out, it's the key to marketing.

Personalized marketing, that's how it is in the twenty-first century.

You don't market on social media, you engage! You are charming and witty and friendly. You're funny. You don't tweet about fiction. (Even if, like me, your entire life revolves around fiction.)

So what if you're an introvert — push harder, step outside your box (clearly suggested by an extrovert because every introvert knows she is not sitting inside a box at all. It has nothing to do with a damn box.)

If you think you can just do what you love — write fiction — you are clueless, they say. You need to market and sell, you need to look after your business. True. I must do those things, but I mostly want to write fiction, and I absolutely do not want to promote my books, chasing down reviewers, and going on blog tours, and tweeting wit. (Is Twitter called by that name because the environment is built around wit, so its very name encompasses the word?)

I'm not witty. Occasionally I suppose some wit leaks out, but it's certainly not off the cuff. I'm thoughtful and analytical. In fact, that's probably why I'm a writer. I like to think through the things I say, crafting and shaping as I go. I don't hate editing. Two-thirds of the things I intend to say never make it past my lips. By the time I'm finished mentally clarifying my thoughts to be as accurate as possible, the moment has passed.

The notion of *platform* was born in the world of non-fiction. It refers to the people who have benefited from your expertise in a given field, interested people who will ask you to speak on the topics you know in depth, who will buy books you've written on those topics — from real estate to religion.

When agents and publishers start talking about platforms for fiction writers, the legs of those theoretical platforms can be quite hollow. If you write funny, entertaining blogs and humorous fiction, great. But what if your blog is very funny and your fiction not so much?

What if you are witty on Twitter but you write historical fiction that has no place for what's considered clever in the twenty-first century?

Historical fiction writers can blog about and gain history buff followers. But even that can be a narrow bridge. History buffs don't necessarily and often do not like to read fiction. They like to read history.

Those who write themed cozy mysteries can blog about food or knitting or dogs. That probably works.

But despite the reams of suggestions on this topic — tying blog topics to fiction in a way that attracts your ideal readers — works in only a few cases. For a woman who writes about crime, delving into the mind of a perpetrator with some level of sympathy, blogging about the subject can be quite distasteful. I know, I tried.

Writing literary fiction gives very few avenues for blogging, unless you're going to write about the craft of fiction, and then, your platform turns into a platform of writers, only a few of whom are likely to become fans of your fiction.

Over the years since I first began thinking about how to build this elusive platform I was required to have, the focus has moved away from blogging. Now, it's mostly about Twitter and Instagram followers, Facebook likes and engagement. An even wobblier platform, one with only three legs, the third leg shorter than its companions.

After desperate searches for something that worked, and aborted attempts to build even the smallest platform, I finally began to believe that for most fiction writers, definitely for this one, *fiction* is the platform. If a platform is a group of people who will buy your books, those people are going to be people who like fiction, people who like *your* fiction. Of course, there's the whole getting-them-to-read-what-you've-written bit — a mind-boggling, sometimes seemingly insurmountable problem, a *marketing* problem, but really, fiction is the platform.

With this thought in mind, I attempted to build a platform by writing flash fiction. I posted it weekly to my blog. The response was light and infrequent. Next, I compiled those stories into annual collections, put an excerpt from one of my novels in the back, and lo and behold...a few people bought the books. A smaller few came back and bought the novels. I think. Who knows.

That sort of thing is impossible to measure. I'm sure the ebook stores know, but so far, they aren't saying. Despite living in the age of big data analytics, for an indie fiction writer, it's nearly impossible to connect the dots from marketing to book sales.

My next attempt at building a platform out of fiction was to write the series of novellas I've mentioned. This was back in the era when offering the first book in a series for free was hugely effective in finding new readers. It's still effective, but the struggle to get eyes on that first free book is not insignificant. Back then, free books were a novelty.

I planned to follow the advice that I release books more frequently, offering the built-in appeal of a series character. With a novella-length book, I could write a book every two-to-three months. Unfortunately, life got in the way, and there were several lags in my release schedule. By the time I finished the series, there were thousands, hundreds of thousands of free books out there. More books than anyone could read in a lifetime.

Still, I pressed forward — writing novels, building a platform made out of fiction, brick-by-brick, knowing that as readers *slowly* find my work, there will be more books for those who become fans.

Fiction is a fiction writer's platform. That's all.

I'm A Person, Not A Brand

Originality is everything in writing fiction, in all artistic endeavors.

Letting your own voice take center stage is crucial.

Writing what your passionate about is crucial.

Doing it your way is crucial.

You are all there is.

It's hard to read about marketing without stumbling across a lot of discussion over branding. Often, this means the look and feel of book covers — font, image, color, adherence to genre conventions. It's focused on how those cover designs tie into your website, social media, and your advertising.

Thinking of branding in terms of the appearance of a writer's book covers, web page, social media style is like choosing a partner based on his looks, her personality at parties, and the decor in her house.

These things draw attention. It's important for your books to communicate visually the kind of story they are. It's important to have the various pieces of your online presence fit together.

But brand is about what readers expect from you. Not what they're initially drawn to. It's about why they like *your* writing and prefer *your* books over others. It's about what's inside the cover.

Customers loyal to a brand such as Disney aren't in love with the look of the characters, the themes of the movies, or the visual impression of the rides at the amusement parks. They are loyal to the experience Disney has given them. They love the memories of visits to the parks, the entertainment and emotions offered by the movies. When they purchase Disney-themed clothing or jewelry, they're expressing their love for particular characters that Disney brought to life. They adore the fact that animated creatures have taken on larger-than-life personas as if they're human beings, friends even.

Good brands provide an experience. That's what generates loyalty.

Readers loyal to a fiction brand such as Lee Child aren't consciously aware of what his book covers communicate, or what he says in interviews, or what his website looks like. I wonder how many readers have never visited his website. Readers who love Lee Child actually love Jack Reacher, the character he created. When a brand is as successful as the Jack Reacher brand, people veer close to the edge of thinking and talking as if Jack were a flesh and blood human being.

Readers enraptured by Kristin Hannah love her writing style and her stories. If you put them into an empty room, how many would be able to describe the covers? Would they remember the font used for her name and book title? It's the worlds she creates, the stories she tells, the way she manages language like a maestro, and the characters who come to life and strike an emotional chord in the hearts of readers.

You build your brand by being you. Yes, some attention needs to be paid to the visual representation of your imagination, but readers will not fall in love with your books because of a stunning cover. They won't look for your next novel because of your chatter on Twitter or your breathtaking or charming photographs on Instagram. They want your stories, your characters. They want the view of the world that emerges from *your* imagination and takes shape in the words you write and the stories you weave out of nothing into something lifelike.

That's a brand. And it only comes from deep within the writer. In some ways, it's you, at your very core, not the face in your mirror.

Home On the Web

There needs to be a place on the world wide web that you call home, where readers can find you and find out about your books and more about how to engage with you — a place that's your own that isn't just a digital store window.

Some writers believe Facebook or your Amazon author profile is sufficient. And technically, it is. Readers can find out about your books, sign up for your newsletter, or chat with you. But those places are owned by someone else. Facebook and Amazon are allowing you to set up a bookcase in their home. But it's their home. They decide how your books are displayed. They are an ever-present third wheel in your interactions with your readers.

But I chose independent publishing, and I want a place where I'm in charge.

A home on the web can be as simple as a blog built on a free site or as spectacular as a revolving shelf of 3D books.

In my effort to built my corner of the internet, I went through multiple iterations of my website. The first lived on a simple template provided by Google. After a while, I needed more than just some flat pages. I moved to a WordPress blog and spent quite a bit of time spiffing it up to look like a website. It was fun, I know a little HTML, and that helped. I liked trying to figure out how to make it look somewhat unique. Rearranging the decor inside my online home every few months was fun and satisfying. It still is. If I had time, I'd probably be moving the furniture and artwork every year.

From the blog, I transitioned to a provider that allowed me to have additional control over the structure. I thought I was super-sophisticated with all these technical capabilities that I sort of understood. Sort of. It sometimes took hours to implement changes, but I figured it was worth it. I was in charge.

Then, on Christmas Eve 2012, I received an email from a writer I'd never met, virtually or otherwise. He informed me that the footer on my website was transmitting links to shopping and porn sites. He sent a link to a screenshot of my home page. (See why I remember the exact date?!)

I spent ten minutes researching him to be sure he wasn't on some sort of phishing expedition of his own. I looked at his screenshot in horror, then I looked at my website. It appeared to be fine. Next came a test with another browser and an accelerating pulse rate and thoughts of the Christmas Eve dinner I needed to prepare and the guests arriving in two hours. I contemplated opening the wine early.

I sent frantic email to my hosting company. While I waited for a response, I researched hacking. The helpful writer had known enough about websites to tell me it was probably my template causing the problem and it needed an update. I never made updates to my template because I'd customized the code and the one time I updated, everything was written over. And of course, I kept terrible records of my customizations because they were all produced by stumbling around in a sea of inscrutable commands, crying *Eureka*, and moving on to the next step without noting what I'd done while I was creating my original website.

I finally found a helpful hint on what might be allowing some dark spirit to control my site, deleted the offending line, and all appeared to be well.

Then I received email from my typically unhelpful hosting company. In fairness, it's not their job to teach me how to develop websites, but since I was paying a monthly fee, I expected *something*. After reading their list of suggestions decipherable only to a software developer, I came to their final point – *We suggest hiring someone who knows what they're doing.* They were right, but I bristled. And so I took their suggestion. Bye-bye hosting company.

I found a terrific organization — small, only three employees — who provided design, development, and website hosting. They were a wonderful group of people. It took just a single one-hour phone call for them to totally get my style, my taste, and what I wanted to communicate. When they were done, I had a gorgeous new site that I could update myself. When something more significant needed attention, they were right there.

Then another tremor ran beneath the foundation of my web home.

My developer informed me they were going out of business. They graciously allowed months for me to find a new home. In the midst of this, I met some new neighbors who provided marketing, social media, and website support for a variety of local businesses. They said they had some great ideas for marketing my work locally. They would also help develop a new site, all for a reasonable fee.

I signed up for a three-year contract with the hosting company they recommended, and the prep for the website migration began.

And then, their daughter was killed in a car accident. I was horrified and sick with imagining the depth of their grief. I knew I couldn't approach them, and of course, for nearly two years, I was not on their radar at all.

I took long walks thinking about how they'd had their hearts ripped out. I hurt for them. I pushed away thoughts of something so horrible happening to me as I imagined their pain. I'd only met these people twice. We'd had a great meeting, felt a strong connection, then exchanged a few emails.

Beyond the usual conventions, how do you express sympathy to someone you've started to know but don't really? I'd seen their daughter once. Along with every inexplicable thing in the world, I couldn't comprehend why this happened to them.

After six months mired in the capricious nature of life, I had to do something because I'd long overstayed my welcome with the original developer.

I located another local developer. He pointed out that my site wasn't mobile-friendly and I really needed a re-design. I couldn't afford what he quoted, so I asked him to simply migrate what I had.

Through a series of personal issues he was dealing with, and some de-prioritizing of my low-cost requirements, we went around in circles for several months. I got frustrated.

One morning I woke up and decided I needed a new website. Now. I didn't want to be dependent on developers. In the years since I'd first built a WordPress blog, the platform had improved significantly, including designs that automatically adapted to mobile use.

I chose a template, learned how to work with the new interface, and designed my own. I saved every piece of my existing site in PDF and built a simpler site. I had fun digging back into the hands-on work of designing something that pleased me, stretching my brain to develop new skills. I pay a reasonable fee for the business plan which gives me personal support when I need it, which is rare.

My website isn't as slick as I'd like. And someday, I know I'll hire a firm to build me a custom home. But for now, it works beautifully on mobile phones, where over half my readers spend their time. It features all my work on the home page, and it's easy to find your way around.

I'm in control. No porn can invade my site, it's automatically backed up, and readers can find me and my books in an attractive virtual home.

Kindle Unlimited: Devil or Angel?

Amazon's Kindle Unlimited program is controversial. I've held every possible opinion regarding the value and risk of offering my books to readers who pay $9.99 a month for access to thousands of books, most of them self-published.

When I first started working on this book, I wrote this harsh statement —

Writers' success in KU is based on being locked into Amazon. Their ranking is based on something other than an actual sale. Pricing is taken out of their control because the rate of pay varies every month at Amazon's whim. I can see why a lot of writers earning a lot of money in the program refuse to believe that they are doing themselves a disservice by allowing this to happen. They want to believe it will last forever. They want to believe Amazon will continue to make it beneficial for them.

This almost looks quaint after years of issues and changes with KU that I won't go into here. There are reams of discussion threads on KBoards about the challenges and the varying opinions of the program and how beholden it makes a writer to Amazon. If you do a Google search, you'll find enough information to keep you reading for the rest of the day.

I finally decided to try it out. I was frustrated with my lack of visibility, my marketing failures.

I put several of my novels into the program. As of this writing, Kindle Unlimited requires exclusivity, which is one of the ways a writer is ceding control to Amazon. But visibility seemed like a fair exchange.

I had a flurry of page reads for about a week, and then nothing. It looked like it wasn't going to give me the visibility it gave to others after all. The minute my three-month term ended, I yanked the books out and once again made them available for sale in other ebook stores.

Shortly after this, Amazon rolled out a pay-per-click advertising program which was available only to KU participants. I put a few books into the program again in order to take advantage of the advertising. Results from my ads were very good. I put the rest of my books into the program.

I hated that I was beholden to Amazon for a varying pay rate. I hated that my books weren't available on whatever platform readers chose. But I was selling books and my books were being read. Books that had only had two or three sales in their entire lives were downloaded and read every week.

It also nagged at me that I was making about what I would make on a book priced at $2.99. My books are $3.99 and $4.99, which we finally settled on as a fair and reasonable price for an ebook. But the lower royalty from Kindle Unlimited was, and is, counter-productive to my effort to make a living as a fiction writer.

I didn't like not knowing how many people read my books all the way through and how many quit a few chapters in. Although I comforted myself that I don't know that when I sell a book either.

Advertising became increasingly expensive, and eventually, Amazon Advertising was offered to all publishers. More about that in a few chapters.

For those who haven't been up to their eyeballs in the self-publishing world, there were issues with scammers using the program in ways that damaged legitimate writers. If you search the internet for Kindle Unlimited Scams, you'll learn more than you ever wanted to know. I stayed in KU and still have my books available there in December 2018. It's still not my first choice, but…it has helped readers find my books.

The best, most thrilling aspect of Kindle Unlimited is that not only have thousands of readers discovered my fiction, many of them have become enthusiastic, loyal, supportive, cheering fans. They make all of this more fun and more satisfying than I ever imagined, even in all of my dreaming.

No matter what its problems and the risk I'm taking publishing my ebooks exclusively with Amazon, those readers mean everything to me. I am incredibly grateful. Sometimes, when I stop to think about how that program introduced readers to my work, it's almost too good to be true.

It's a dream come true.

Cover Madness

All my obsession and second-guessing over the choices I made for my book covers have truly boarded on madness.

When I started self-publishing, there weren't cover designers opening up shop in every corner of the internet like they are now. There wasn't a lot of discussion about book covers in those early days. The Kindle had been out for three years, and Amazon had just announced they would split ebook revenue in a seventy/thirty deal for books priced $2.99 to $9.99, favoring the author.

The wave of enthusiasm for self-publishing began to swell, and the term *indie author* was coined as writers proudly chose to publish their own work and wanted a descriptor that evoked the idea of independent filmmakers and musicians.

The conversation was about the suddenly real possibility that more writers could make a living with their fiction, and about getting your work out to an audience that you could find and develop yourself. It was about readers finding your books on Amazon. It was about whether ebooks should be priced at $.99 or $2.99.

As best I recall, the focus on the importance of professional book covers came later.

Most of that conversation focuses on covers that fit the expectations of genre. And here was my genre problem. Again.

I didn't want traditional thriller covers because my books are not traditional thrillers. Readers who picked up one of my novels expecting a traditional thriller would be disappointed. I didn't want paranormal-style covers for my ghost stories because my books are far afield from the hot paranormal categories.

Excited about having absolute creative control, I started out using photographs staged by me and captured by people I knew. It was fun to imagine an object or scene from my novel or novella and create an image with the modeling and photography help of friends and family.

Soon, it became clear these were adequate but not compelling.

I moved to using stock photography, finding images that evoked the theme or a character in the novel.

But I worried. I wanted them to stand out among other thrillers, so the difference was evident at a glance, but did they stand out too much?

I looked at traditionally published books that were more mainstream but still in the psychological thriller category. Mine looked indistinguishable on the shelf. They fit in and stood out at the same time.

Then I would read yet another KBoards thread or a blog post about the absolutely critical importance of a cover that told readers what kind of book they were getting. These directives and threads stated that if a writer's books aren't selling, the first place she should look is her cover. They insisted the cover had to meet expectations.

But what expectations?

I combed through Amazon. I spent hours, enough hours that they added up to days, downloading covers and lining them up beside mine, scrutinizing every font and color and image.

With a few of my books, I decided the cover needed to be changed. I had one modified to look like other thriller covers. Sales remained the same for that book — close to zero. Only when I started advertising the novel did that change.

Each time I published a book I was madly in love with the cover. When sales didn't meet my hopes and expectations, I questioned the cover, my love still there but very uncertain.

Once again I started my hunt through Amazon, always comparing, constantly questioning.

There's no doubt that book covers influence buying decisions. But there's also no doubt that the so-called perfect book cover is not the master key to finding your audience. A book cover influences some readers to take a closer look, it turns away others. But that's all.

When you're in the book cover market, think about your ideal reader, think about how you want readers to feel about your story, and hire a designer, but don't spend your life searching for that elusive font and face that will launch your book from four sales to four thousand.

To be honest, I didn't relax about my covers until Amazon chose the first book in my psychological suspense series to include in their Prime reading program. (Amazon makes a selection of ebooks available free to Prime members. Books remain in the program for approximately three months. Amazon pays the author a flat fee, and in exchange, your book receives expanded visibility.)

Knowing my cover (not to mention my sub-four-star-review average) made the cut allowed me to relax — a little.

Private Bookstore

A newsletter mailing list is like your own private bookstore, filled with your fans.

If you're drawn to the independent aspect of indie, it can be difficult to run smack into the iron wall that is Amazon or the other ebook stores. Readers can follow writers they like on Amazon, but only Amazon can send them updates, on your behalf, when they choose.

If you want to be the one to tell your readers the book they've been waiting for is here, a mailing list is essential.

There is a lot of advice out there about how to build a mailing list — a *lot* of advice. Writers are told to join with other writers and cross-promote, offering free books that will get fans of other writers to join their own mailing lists. They're advised to run Facebook ads offering a free book to entice people to sign up. Some writers put newsletter sign-up invites in both the front and the back of their books. (This one perplexes me. I wouldn't be inclined to sign up for a newsletter before I read the book, but that's me.)

These techniques didn't work for me. First, the genre misfit thing, which I won't go on about yet again.

The other reason these suggestions didn't work may also be related to genre. Some newsletter strategies, such as soliciting interaction through surveys and contests work better in some genres than others. The effectiveness of marketing techniques varies by genre.

As with everything, you have to find what works for you and your books, and that's what makes this process so very slow and painful. Some writers figure out right away what works for them. Clearly, I'm not one of those writers.

One book that was helpful and gave me a new perspective on newsletters is *Newsletter Ninja* by Tammi Labrecque. This book doesn't advocate randomly signing up anyone who will take a free book as some suggest. Not all of the suggestions worked for me, but some did. The book does a great job focusing your attention on readers as human beings rather than names to add to a list.

Modifying advice as I seem prone to do, I tried giving away a free story instead of a novel as part of a Facebook ad. I thought new readers might get to it sooner and get hooked sooner than they would with a novel. That ad was very inexpensive because there were very few clicks on my offer.

After a little over two years writing a series, close to two hundred people have signed up to find out when I release new books. I cherish every single one of those readers. They came slowly, but they've stayed. And they like reading my books.

There's a simple request in the back of my books telling them if they'd like to hear from me on a monthly basis with occasional discounts and most importantly, when a new novel is available. Every month, a handful, sometimes two handfuls, sign up.

That's enough for me.

A mild, organic approach fits my personality. I issue an invitation, and that's enough. I'm not going to badger readers into coming to my party, just to watch them have a miserable time and try to sneak out early. I'd much rather enjoy the company of those who are thrilled to be there.

Mad Men

Advertising has been around as long as human beings have been selling something they've made to others. Mad Men glamorized it. Amazon capitalized on it.

Writers want to write fiction, not ad copy, but here we are. This is reality.

I could write a book about my advertising experiences. Many authors have written books about how to effectively advertise fiction. We've purchased a fair number of them, and still, we're struggling and learning. We've been advertising on Amazon for over two years, and we're still struggling and learning.

We've put together something that works for my novels, sort of, by using information in a few books and mud-wrestling with thousands of columns and rows of spreadsheets filled with Amazon data.

If you want to learn more about advertising, I recommend starting with David Gaughran who has written three books about self-publishing and marketing fiction. I recommend him because he's extremely knowledgeable and funny, always a bonus. He provides a lot of information on his blog and through his newsletter. Sadly, none of his recommendations have worked for me, but he did make me think differently about imagining my ideal reader. His suggestions have worked for many, many writers. So check him out. And he's funny.

When I first started self-publishing, advertising wasn't such a thing. There were newsletters that were sent to Kindle reader subscription lists promoting your book for a reasonable fee. We used some of these and saw small bumps of twenty to thirty sales.

As the shelves of Amazon filled to overflowing, advertising became more of a necessity, and now, it's a requirement in most cases.

All the things that had worked for indie author marketing prior to that have faced a glut of writers over the years — blogging, social media, giveaways, chatting in forums. It's entirely possible those things still work for some, but they were always minimally effective for me and never led to a building a solid audience.

After a monumental struggle, Amazon Advertising began to work for me. It's what made the difference between occasional random spurts in the midst of woefully low sales and seeing steady sales and the reaction of more readers falling in love with my novels.

When I get bogged down in the minutia of writing ad copy and checking cost-per-click and all the other details, I try to step back and marvel at what a great opportunity it is. Using the pages of the largest bookstore on the planet, writers can put a teaser for their books in front of readers. You're not fighting with clothing and vacation ads. Just books! And you don't have to spend a cent unless someone is interested and clicks on your ad.

It's a fantastic opportunity that I try to keep focused on rather than the daily grind of working with a cumbersome system and a certain lack of transparency.

A large number of writers have effectively used Facebook ads to reach readers. There are lots of resources out there for learning how to use them effectively. They didn't work for me. And in the end, I love the idea of advertising solely to readers.

We spent too much while we're on a learning curve, but we did find readers who enjoy my books. And slowly, we've managed to wrestle it under some semblance of control.

Some of my insight into making Amazon Ads work for me came from Brian Meeks' book — *Mastering Amazon Ads.*

Although his bidding cost information is out of date, if you want to understand how certain types of Amazon Ads work, it's worth a read. The book helped me understand how to approach advertising on Amazon overall and emphasized the importance of learning to write good ad copy. All well worth the investment. And he's funny.

One point he makes repeatedly is that you need to experiment. And I can echo the importance of testing and experimenting. All of our mistakes and missteps and mess-ups resulted in unintended experimentation, which brought us closer to making the ads work for us.

Unfortunately, it's very difficult for your books to be discovered without advertising. There are over five million ebooks on Amazon at this point in time. I don't let that discourage me too frequently. Millions of those books have never sold more than a copy or two, some have never sold at all.

But when people proclaim your book isn't selling because you need a new cover…step back and consider how easy it is to find your book. And then let the experimenting begin.

I spent money I shouldn't have, but if you start slowly, remain patient, and move forward carefully, it's possible to generate income to cover advertising expenses.

Join the Party

Advice abounds that social media is the way to build your platform, a free way to promote your books, a tool you must master, forums where you must participate, parties you can't miss, a way that you must engage with readers. But when you don't yet have readers, this is demoralizing in the extreme.

I've repeated a lot of common experiences and beliefs about social media. It's a time sink. It can damage creativity if it's not kept in its place.

Advice on platform building seems to skip over the fact that it's social. Meaning it's not where you stand on the corner dressed as a chicken and wave an ad banner. But some readers do want to engage with writers, and like a chicken and its egg, once you have readers, they'll get in touch with you in their preferred manner, often through their favorite form of social media.

Social media, for me, for most writers I'm aware of, does not work for finding readers, for relentlessly promoting books, despite all the advice to the contrary. I still occasionally see agents touting the importance of getting Twitter followers. One advised new writers should start building a presence on Twitter by following agents and their clients.

When I have a new book, I announce it once on social media. My readers respond. That's all.

Chicken and egg.

A Long-term relationship

Successful indie authors will insist you must write a series. A series gets readers hooked into your books. After the first book, the rest of the books in a series sell themselves. Readers crave series.

Maybe you're thinking — that's not for me. That's not what I read. Literary fiction and mainstream novels usually come in one complete story, possibly in a trilogy. The thrillers I like feature an epic story from start to finish. But a character that keeps going? Someone who has multiple stories? That's not what I usually read.

Or maybe you're thinking you'll get bored writing about the same character through eight or ten or twenty novels.

This was my mindset for years. Mostly the first one...I don't read a lot of series. When I was growing up, I read about Perry Mason and Hercule Poirot and Judy Bolton. But as an adult, not so much. I can't explain why. As much as I love Ruth Rendell's standalone novels, I never became a fan of her Inspector Wexford series. I read a few. I liked them, but I had no desire to follow the character. I liked the side characters and the twisting plots more than I liked Wexford.

It seemed crass to write a series simply because that's what sells. It seemed as if I wouldn't be following my own creative bent. I thought I would have to force the character to life.

After I published my first novel, I was impatient for all the indie success I was reading about. I thought my novel would take off and the rest would be bestseller history.

As I worked overtime to publicize my novel, the screaming that I must write a series became so loud, I could hardly think.

Thinking I might write a cozy mystery that *fit the market*, I developed a quirky amateur sleuth who would solve murders in and around the church where she worked. When ghosts appeared in her story and derailed the market fit, I forged ahead. I didn't think I wanted to write a full-blown mystery, so I decided to write novellas. After all, this was self-publishing. Writers were free. We no longer had to be constrained by publishing requirements for certain book lengths. Creativity ruled. The story could be as long or short as the story needed to be.

The series was completed in 2015. Fast-forward several months.

While lying on the couch with a migraine, I was thinking about my irritation over all the books trying to mimic *Gone Girl* by featuring an anonymous "girl". (It didn't start with *Gone Girl*, it just accelerated.) Girls were all over the bookshelves. Women in their 20s, 30s, 40s! All of these adult women called *girls* because the word implied a certain vulnerability and every-woman nature.

I was irritated with an upper case *I*.

As my brain twisted under the piercing pain, a title floated through my mind — *The Woman In the Mirror*. Take that, girls.

I was partially into the second book of my trilogy, wanting to accelerate the action since I'd quit my day job at this point. I decided I would once again try to write to the market. I'd change my quiet suspense style to that of a psychological thriller. It would feature a strong woman who was engaged in a mental battle with her quirky, passive-aggressive and slightly disturbed landlord.

The first three chapters flowed easily out of my fingers as if it had been waiting for years to see the light of day.

And then, during a long walk, a question arose in my mind. Is my protagonist a serial killer? As with all fictional questions and detours, I had no idea where this came from. I went back and read the first chapter. All the seeds were there for a serial killer.

I despaired. Serial killers were not what people wanted to read under the loosely constructed banner of domestic suspense/psychological thriller! Not unless that killer was the villain. Certainly not the heroine that all were supposed to root for!

And again, I chose the passion of my creative voice over what might sell.

Once the character revealed herself, my mind was flooded with titles about Women — *The Woman In the Water, Painting, Window, Bar, Bedroom*...

Part of the creative fun came from asking myself at the start of each novel — Who is the "everywoman" in this story?

Suddenly, I was writing a series. It didn't start out that way. Maybe my subconscious was working away, fed by years of hearing and ignoring this advice. Maybe it was meant to be. Maybe I just found a character that couldn't be contained in a single novel. I'll never know.

As I began to think about the idea of series characters, trying to understand why I hadn't been drawn to them, I realized that I had, just not in the novels I chose.

The TV shows I was addicted to were appealing for just that reason. I loved the characters and wanted to see them episode after episode, season after season, grieving for them when their stories ended.

Six Feet Under. The Shield. Damages. Homicide. Breaking Bad. Better Call Saul. Happy Valley. House of Cards. The Americans. Ozark. The Good Wife. I could go on. I highly recommend every single one of those shows. The characters are brilliant. The stories are gripping. Those shows lifted me out of my own life and helped me live in another world. The writing and story-telling go well beyond anything network TV offered in years past.

Clearly, I liked series more than I'd realized. Maybe I just hadn't tried enough of them to find a series of novels I loved.

In the end, the advice worked for me.

Writing a series is what allowed me to build a core group of readers who love my work. Not only do they read and plead for the release of the next book (a gift that I'm overwhelmed by every day), many of them read my other novels as well.

When a reader finds a writer to her or his liking, there aren't enough books in print to satisfy their desire for more. If you think a series isn't for you, let that thought settle into your subconscious. Something surprising might emerge.

Kindle Unlimited, book covers, a newsletter, advertising, reviews, and social media. Every single one of those things started clicking in after I started writing a series.

One final word on marketing. Sometimes we think we're forcing our books into readers' lives. But really, marketing is simply introducing readers to books we know they'll love.

A STORY WITH NO ENDING

What Readers Want

Visibility and reader awareness are challenges for almost everyone outside the top 10-20 percent, whether traditionally or self-published. The good news is that as an indie author, the English-reading world is your audience. And once you're established, it's not limited to English.

As tablets and smart-phones settle themselves permanently into the center of our lives, that audience continues to solidify. As the indie wave continues swelling, I keep learning about more writers who will never be famous or have Publisher's Weekly articles written about them. They aren't on the New York Times or USA Today bestseller lists, and they aren't ranked in the top twenty on Amazon. Yet, they have readers who devour every book they write, and they're earning good to great to amazing money. They quit their day jobs and are living their dream career.

Their names aren't known, but they've satisfied their readers with enough books that they're making a living.

Gimmicks, pricing strategies, social-media "platform" building, newsletter strategies, advertising techniques...all are secondary. Important to consider and adopt, but secondary. What has always worked, and always will?

Writing great stories that a specific group of readers will:

1. love reading

2. want to tell their friends about

and then:

3. presenting those stories coherently as a polished written product.

Do that, and the rest of it will sort itself out.

That was one optimistic writer's opinion on a blog post that's lost in the bits and bytes of the internet. For the most part, I agree. Yes, marketing is a challenge. For me, it's been a monumental challenge. But, that challenge is there whether you self-publish or find a corporation to publish your books.

When you write an amazing book, once a few readers fall in love, you'll have the slow, silent, subterranean, or the rapid, explosive growth that comes from word of mouth. Based on your book. Your imagination. Your view of life. Your characters and the world you created for them. Your words.

The comment above was posted in response to an analysis of how to deconstruct best-selling novels and write your own book to mirror its components in a way that generates similar success.

More comments from the community follow:

There was a tone in the advice that suggested books could be deconstructed and written for a hot genre and sell more than books written out of passion. And that this is a valid, even the advisable route rather than those writing what a writer chooses rather than what readers want, as if the two are mutually exclusive.

And another voice:

They suggest that's the "business" side, that this is a job and you must write what the market wants. This is true, but the market wants cheap phones. They also want and will pay for iPhones.

It seems fitting that the iPhone is mentioned here. Former Apple CEO and iPhone creative genius Steve Jobs famously said, "People don't know what they want until we give it to them."

That is the point of the visionary, the market leader, the best-seller...The writer who sets trends rather than chases them. Gillian Flynn, at the urging of her husband, wrote the book she wanted to write. She let it rip. For six years and counting, publishers have been trying to find the next *Gone Girl,* and many writers have been trying to create it.

Great fiction takes risks

On many industry blogs, the conversation sounds like giddy high schoolers talking about the prom. *What should I write? How should I write it? What's hot right now?* To me, the tone sounds like some ephemeral magical formula is more important than intelligent writing and interesting stories. Many of those conversations are lightweight, everyone parroting the same beliefs back and forth, afraid to take risks, afraid to follow their creative voice. Ironically, great art of any kind, including great books, requires creativity, risk and the willingness to be different. It requires a human connection that I don't believe is found in paint-by-number books. It requires a willingness to offend when necessary.

Quoting Stephen King (*again*), "If you expect to succeed as a writer, rudeness should be the second-to-least of your concerns. The least of all should be polite society and what it expects. If you intend to write as truthfully as you can, your days as a member of polite society are numbered, anyway."

"There are two or three human stories, and they go on repeating themselves as fiercely as if they had never been told before." — Willa Cather

In other words, and I can't say it enough, it's your voice. Readers want *your* voice.

Is This A Career?

I became a writer when I was a child. I wanted to lift the thoughts out of my skull, ink them onto sheets of paper, and inspect them. Or something like that. I wanted to do for other readers what my favorite writers had done for me. Transport me into the midst of other lives. Maybe part of the desire to read is to see the complete arc of a life because we can never see our own.

At some point, those desires turn into thoughts of wanting a career writing fiction.

That was not a *legitimate* career. Writing was a dream, a hobby, an avocation.

A career is meant to put food on the table and a roof over your head. As you move into your twenties, a career is meant to provide health insurance and savings for old age. It's important to find work you enjoy, but you don't pick something you love to do and set off with the mindset that it will provide financial stability. Or financial anything.

A serious person looks at the possible fields of work and finds one that fits their interests and temperament.

When I first submitted short stories and wrote columns for local papers, I wanted my work to be read. On another level, I wanted the validation that comes with publication. I wanted to know that I was a "good enough" writer to be "published". Others not only chose to read what I wrote, they liked it enough to put it in their newspaper or magazine.

I have no idea why this was important. Maybe when you put time and energy into any pursuit, you want other people to notice. Writing is communication and what is communication without a receiving party on the other end?

All along I knew that writing fiction was not a way to earn an income. I absorbed this idea from our culture in general which promotes the notion that art is a hobby, an outlet, an avenue for self-realization. As I started writing more and reading about what it takes to get published, I was hammered with messages that less than five percent of writers earn a living from their fiction, that most books only sell a few hundred copies.

It takes a lot of hubris to decide you're going to be in that five percent. And when I first moved my sights toward writing for publication, I don't think I necessarily expected that. I was more focused on seeing my novels on bookstore shelves and in libraries and readers' hands.

The story of my migration from pursuing traditional publishing and the associated dreams with all my heart to deciding to self-publish is the story of wanting a career. I didn't want to teach and write fiction. I didn't want to work in high tech and write fiction. I didn't want to be supported by my husband and write fiction. I wanted a self-supporting career.

Possibly only five percent of traditionally published writers do make a living from their writing. That sounds about right. The stories I've heard of writers being dropped by their publisher and evidence of decreasing advances, a trickle of royalties suggest that's the case.

But in the twenty-first century, you can make a living writing fiction. If you self-publish. If you recognize it's not easy. It takes time and patience and publishing several books before you have enough work to advertise cost-effectively.

Some writers madly pursue that desire to make money, to the exclusion of what they really want to write. Some need to. They have families to feed and clothe, and they want to write. Some balance the two, finding a popular genre that they enjoy reading.

There are writers who crossed my path in my first year or two of self-publishing who are now well-established, satisfying thousands of fans, and making a good income. There are writers I interacted with who are supporting their families with their fiction.

When you're earning an income doing what you love, when you're seeing your books purchased and read every day, when you're hearing from readers that they can't wait for your next novel, all that desire for validation and seeing your paperback in a bookstore dissolves.

If you have doubts that you can make a living doing what you love, you can find all the details you want through Author Earnings. The data analyst who produces these reports uses bots to gather regular sales rank data and other information form ebook stores. From this, he extrapolates earnings for writers at various points in their careers, both traditionally and self-published.

Maybe having a full-time career is not your dream. Maybe you want a part-time income because you love your day job and you also love writing. Maybe you have any one of a hundred other desires. In that case, self-publishing is still the more likely avenue to getting your work into the hands of readers than playing the lottery that traditional publishing has become — hoping an agent thinks your work has commercial potential, hoping a publisher agrees, hoping their assessment is correct, hoping that commercial potential is still there in eighteen months when the book steps out into the daylight, hoping that you have the resources to market your work to their satisfaction, hoping your first novel does well enough that they're willing to offer you a contract for a second, and a third…

It's been hard watching others reach the goals I dream of in half the time, while I strain to make it to the next rung on the ladder, but the information in Author Earnings, and the mild success I've had so far keep me going every day. I want my work to be read, and I want to support myself pursuing the only career I ever really wanted.

Momentum & Mistakes

The number of mistakes I've made building a career as a fiction writer is too large to count. I think it's safe to say I made fistfuls of mistakes in every single area of writing and marketing and maintaining my equilibrium. And I don't undervalue maintaining equilibrium. Without that, everything else falls apart.

I also can't count the number of times I told my husband that it would just be nice to see some momentum. By that, I meant a steady increase in sales. And I wasn't ignorant enough to think that would be a straight line, shooting up and to the right of the chart. Of course, there would be fluctuations, but couldn't we have some kind of upward trajectory?

Looking back, I have a bit of that now, I suppose. Sales are relatively steady, and the number of readers who want to read future novels is increasing.

Advertising is still an enormous challenge.

In 2018, we sold enough books to generate a livable income. Except for the ads. The outflow in advertising costs left us with a profit for the year, but the profit is not a livable income. By any stretch. Yet.

I made mistakes in the amount of money I spent on ads and the amount of time I spent freaking out over bad reviews. The first is something I can control. The second I can't do anything about. I'm learning to focus on what I can control, wondering why that's been such a difficult lesson for me.

I made mistakes with book covers, formatting, and copyediting. Mistakes abounded in my interaction with the online world and the advice I took to heart without analyzing whether said advice consisted of an opinion and a personal experience rather than a broadly applicable principle.

It was a mistake not to start a series sooner, but at the same time, that series was born organically rather than something I forced due to a desire to accelerate my success.

There were tons of mistakes in pricing — mostly pricing too low and thinking that would, again, accelerate my progress. For me, pricing novels at ninety-nine cents, and even at $2.99 made no discernible difference in sales. And yet I can't recall how many times I looked at sales, felt discouraged, and rushed to lower prices across the entire catalog of books.

When I read in one of Kristine Kathryn Rusch's blog posts that it takes ten years to establish a career as a fiction writer, I wailed with frustration. I didn't want to wait ten years. I'd already put in a good ten years learning how to write, practicing my craft, finding my voice that was buried beneath piles of decaying leaves. Yet, here I am, eight years and counting.

Others have achieved success much faster, so maybe it's just me. But I don't think it is. I think those with rapid success fall into two categories. Some had a brief stint in the traditional world which gave them a fan base to start with. Others are skilled marketers. Others were lucky. But I think they're the exception. I don't think I'm alone in taking a very, *very* long time to get where I want to go.

In all of this desire for momentum, the yearning to make writing fiction a full-time career, the biggest mistake I made was not writing. When I think of all the hours I spent following angst-filled diatribes about people gaming Amazon, or having public melt-downs in response to vicious reader reviews, or arguing about the *right way* to build a writing career, I would have written twice the number of novels over those years. And that would have given me more of the momentum I long for.

Writers write. It doesn't mean they're hacks when they write a lot of books. It means they're prolific. That they're *writers*.

I would have had a lot more fun and a whole lot more equilibrium if I'd spent more time writing.

Instead of looking for the secret, thinking there even *is* a secret to a successful career as a writer, I would have done what works. Write.

I Can't Get No Satisfaction

The *Opportunity* section of this book offered a high-level overview of marketing and sales and finding an audience. But the title of the book is *Writing* is Murder.

I included those other facets because they're all part of being a writer who wants to get her work into the hands of readers. Climbing those mountains is something only the rarefied few escape.

Why is writing murder? I said at the start of this book — a writer has to suffocate her critical voice in order to get into the creative flow, stab her ego in the heart to get feedback, and drown her self-doubt in order to put her work out into the world. If you're not careful, some of those activities can kill you with the effort required and the frustration endured. But if you like to write, if you're driven to write, there are only a few things more pleasurable on earth.

For me, writing is mind-expanding. When I let go and allow my mind to travel where it chooses, like a rushing creek after a storm, cutting through new terrain, taking the direction it chooses, it's another plane of existence.

Writing is sometimes like the eerie trip people seek in psychedelic drugs without the damaging effects. Fantastical and absolutely mind-expanding.

"We write in order not just to be read, but to read – texts not yet written, which only we can bring into being." —Joyce Carol Oates

I've struggled with how to write for myself, for my own pleasure, finding satisfaction in the work, especially during the revision and editing process when it's not quite so *mind-expanding*.

It's what Ms. Oates said. I write to read something that tells a story that satisfies me with characters, with imagined life experiences that become as real as my own, with language. I imagine inner worlds that are nothing like mine and some that are quite similar to mine. I experience stories that wouldn't exist, and I wouldn't get to read if I didn't write them.

When I keep my mind on that — I'm happy. Sales or not. And marketing seems woefully unimportant, something that must be done, like vacuuming or dusting or scrubbing toilets, and not something that I need to freak out over. Marketing is simply letting readers know your book is out there — extremely simple and heartbreakingly complex. But focusing on the simple and not getting sucked into all the so-called *new and proven* techniques *guaranteed* to fulfill all your dreams helps preserve your sanity and your life.

Letting Go

Write a series. Publish books every two months. Tweet. Don't tweet. Write without an outline. Plot first. Stick to one genre. Expand to several genres. Brand yourself. Advertise. Advertising doesn't work. Hire an editor. Traditional publishers don't really edit anymore, you just need a proofreader. Make sure your cover fits your genre. Make sure your cover is unique. Make sure your cover fits your brand. Make sure your cover stands out. Make sure your cover echoes others.

Write short blurbs. Write detailed blurbs. Write what you love to read. Make sure you write books in the genres the market loves. Get an agent. Agents don't add value. Write in the morning. Write at night. No one buys short stories. Write more short stories. No one buys novellas. Novellas are the perfect form for ebooks. Join a critique group. Don't take their critiques to heart, in fact, avoid them. Find your voice, you are your voice. Find your tribe, target your readers, blog about your fictional world. Write fast. Don't rush. Use input from beta readers — but not, definitely *not* the guy you're sleeping with.

Everyone has advice. Everyone knows what works — for them.

It's all enough to make me want to take a very long nap. I don't know the right path, and I don't know the secret to success. I'm pretty sure there is no secret. I do know I love to write fiction and I want to make a living at it. But I can't do a damn thing to make that happen except write and stumble through whatever marketing seems to kinda sorta make my books visible to readers.

I have noticed something remarkable. When I stop checking my reviews and sales statistics and blog hits and retweets... when I release my iron-fisted grip on all that stuff I'm supposed to do...all the stuff I need to do, I have an uptick in sales. Weird and magical and too woo-woo. But it's true.

I'm letting go now. At least for this moment in time.

Writing isn't really murder. Not writing is.

Choking To Death

If I haven't made it ridiculously clear — I've tried it *all*.

To re-cap and some I haven't mentioned: I gave away a Kindle, I ran ads on Kboards, I advertised in newsletters to readers, I made my books free on iTunes and Kobo and through Kindle Select free days. I put excerpts of novels in the backs of my free Flash Fiction. I advertised on GoodReads and Facebook and Amazon. I hosted giveaways on GoodReads. I used BookRooster to get impartial reviews. I leveraged Kirkus Reviews, spending too much money for an impartial review from an industry-recognized organization. I submitted to PW Reviews where my novels were declined. I put requests for reader reviews in the backs of my books and then I didn't. I wrote a series and made the first one free. I wrote another series. I sent my books to book bloggers.

I submitted short stories to literary magazines and suspense magazines. I entered contests. I participated in online Flash Fiction forums.

I changed several covers. I re-wrote blurbs a stupid number of times. I adjusted keywords and categories, sometimes monthly.

I tweeted. I posted on Facebook. I dabbled with Instagram.

I read blogs until my eyes bled and I downloaded free pamphlets on the secrets to marketing. I bought books about marketing. I bought packages that bundled multiple books on marketing into one breathtaking package of tips and strategies guaranteed to work.

I started a mailing list and solicited sign-ups.

I swallowed so much advice, I almost choked to death.

Through it all, I wrote more books.

And then I went local.

I began writing a trilogy set around a beloved local landmark. I sold books on consignment at a local bookstore, and I signed books at a church holiday faire. I asked and was welcomed to put out a container of bookmarks at several local businesses where I was a regular customer. Two of the books in the trilogy are set in the past, so I placed bookmarks at the local history museum. I sent press releases to local papers and community news blogs.

The bookstore requested a proposal outlining my marketing plan and my ideas for a book signing. Then they declined to host one. They said they might do a joint signing with several local authors. They didn't.

I promoted the local bookstore on my website. I tweeted about them. I bought books and attended readings there. I sold books at the bookstore. I still do — a handful a month. Readers return for the other books in the trilogy.

The bookstore put up a suburban noir display and promoted all my novels for a month. Ultimately, I sold truckloads more copies of the trilogy on Amazon.

Advice is available everywhere. For me, I've often gotten so caught up in advice-taking, I've lost sight of who I am. Many times, I didn't think critically about the advice I was given.

I have bits of advice sprinkled throughout this book, but I have no idea whether it will work for you. Finding an audience and making a living in the arts is difficult. At the same time, the opportunity for fiction writers now is greater than it's ever been. The entire planet is at our fingertips.

There are millions of books. But there are *billions* of people. Of course, that number is reduced significantly when taking into account the number of people who read English, but for me, the vastness remains the same — incomprehensible. And that gives me hope, which I often need much more than I need advice.

Don't Quit Your Day Job

Everyone says — Don't quit your day job...

...until you've published seven novels.

...unless you have savings to cover your living expenses for six months...one year...two years...

The milestone of seven traditionally published novels was advice given in a book about building a career as a fiction writer. The book was written in the days when self-publishing was synonymous with vanity publishing, costing thousands of dollars up front and leaving you with a garage full of paperbacks and bolted bookstore doors.

The second is conventional wisdom, and it varies.

The point is, I quit my day job. We had solid savings, and I believed it would take six months until I was making at least half of what we needed to live on.

Instead, it took two and a half years until we became profitable at all. Those were terrifying years. So terrifying it's difficult to put into words. I cried...a LOT.

More often than was healthy, I told my husband to uncork a bottle of wine. Of course, I did that a lot more frequently when I was working in a job I hated, but at least then I didn't agonize over the cost of that bottle while he was turning the corkscrew.

In January of 2015, I first floated the idea of quitting my job. I wanted to put all of my energy and focus into trying to launch a full-time career as a writer. My husband, Mr. Live-In-The-

Moment and Dr. Optimism responded that I should absolutely quit.

I spent eight months re-visiting that decision.

I had a moment of encouragement when out of nowhere, a reader tweeted at me that she loved all my books. Until then, I'd never been contacted directly by a reader. It was a thrill on so many levels. It seemed to me to be some sort of "sign" that my writing career had more potential than I'd believed. It pushed me closer to making the final decision.

I continued to doubt that decision every single week for over three years after I walked out the door, posting a picture of Peggy Olson from Mad Men on my Facebook page. She was walking down the hall after she quit Sterling Cooper. She was carrying a cardboard box filled with the personal items from her office, wearing sunglasses, a cigarette pinched between her lips. Despite my doubts, I felt free and in control, for a moment.

Three things led me to quit.

The first was the death of my father in 2013. He had been fighting the after-effects of aggressive 1960s-style cancer treatments for most of my life. He lived his life to the fullest for over forty years after multiple surgeries, but radiation therapy damaged his intestines. This was followed later by muscle loss that made him dependent on a walker and finally a wheelchair.

I knew for several years that his condition was growing significantly worse. Our family was in pain watching his suffering and in awe of his stoicism and continuing good spirits in the face of his physical difficulties. With all of that, and a week in the hospital as he slipped away, his death was a shock, unlike anything I'd ever experienced. I'd known intellectually that even when you know it's coming, death is shocking in its finality. I'd felt the loss of grandparents, but this was a grief that knocked the breath out of me.

I was suddenly acutely aware of how quickly life passes and how final and sudden the end is.

I didn't want to miss my life. I was working forty-five to fifty hours a week and writing on every holiday and weekend, every morning before work, and every lunch hour. My social life was severely limited and more importantly, my family time was impacted.

My husband is ten years old than I am. How much time did we have left?

I didn't want to live like this.

The second nudge was my job itself. My job had been tolerable for about fifteen years. The work was mildly interesting, most of the time. I had good friends and co-workers. We talked a lot and laughed a lot.

After my company was acquired, I hated my job. Absolutely hated it. I was forced into positions that were a terrible fit for my skills, experience, and personality. First, I worked in an organization that demanded far more technical ability than I had. As a result, I worked seven days a week, 12-14 hours a day (truly) to try to build a knowledge-base that was barely adequate. I burned out after six months and took another position.

In this role, I managed three men who resented being pushed down in the organization, who didn't respect me because of my lack of expertise in sales training and technology. Through a series of management changes, I was put into a job that required intense travel and customer interaction. I had no customer-experience and did not want to spend forty to fifty percent of my time traveling and standing in front of groups of people talking about products I didn't care about or understand in depth.

Because of this, I was given a logistical/planning role with executives who did not like the new management chain where I reported. They were passive-aggressive in working with me. Some outright sabotaged my efforts by giving me incomplete information and then contradicting my reports in large forums in front of senior executives.

While I was waffling with whether I had the courage to put all my trust in my fiction writing, my manager told me more changes were coming. I needed to "re-tool" my career, meaning there were no more analytical roles and I would have to improve my grasp of technology and my ability to sell our products to our customers — global corporations, governments, and huge financial institutions. People who had little patience for marketing fluff and wanted their complex business concerns addressed in a compelling way.

I would be in way, way over my head.

I took it as a "sign", something that's not a good business practice, but in some ways, it *was* a very clear sign. I could either struggle and work health-destroying hours, or I could put my faith in my talent, in my lifelong dream.

The final push came when our neighbor's twelve-year-old daughter was killed in a car accident. The finality and unpredictability of death devastated me.

In a burst of clichés I knew — *it was now or never...life is too short...no guts, no glory.*

Everyone has their own story, their own circumstances. In most cases, I would never advise anyone to do what I did. First of all, I had a husband who was behind me 200%. But a part of me would cheer anyone who took a terrifying risk as I did. On my last day of work, I sent an image to my mother and sisters — Thelma and Louise stomping on the gas and sending their 1966 Ford Thunderbird sailing over the edge of the Grand Canyon. That's how it felt. That's how it feels now.

Thank You for Being My Friend

I am an impatient, demanding, perfectionistic, emotional, and wildly imaginative woman. It's entirely possible this roller coaster ride of self-publishing has been much more chaotic and terrifying than necessary due to my personality.

My husband has the nature of a Zen monk.

When we have a spike in sales, he'll say, "That's great." The tone is even, almost without inflection. His expression is neutral, as it almost always is. I demand to know whether he's excited. In the same smooth tenor voice, he assures me that he is. In my ears, his voice has the tone of someone ordering a cup of coffee.

I would never have had even a sliver of the success I've had without him beside me, reading my books, providing feedback, and working through multiple rounds of edits. Without his sometimes twisted and sometimes lame and sometimes gut-splitting sense of humor, I would have drowned in my own misery years ago.

Having the unfailing and constant support of someone you love is better than writing.

I wish the same for you. And if you don't have that, I hope you can find writer friends who can walk beside you, listening to your story and telling you theirs. I hope this book has let you know you're not alone, and that it's possible to find beloved readers as a self-published author.

Now What?

I didn't set out to persuade you to self-publish, or to tell you how to do it successfully. My goal was to let you know what it's been like for me, and perhaps others who are daily lurkers on blogs and forums and pathological buyers of books about writing and publishing.

I wanted to let you know you aren't alone if you're struggling with the "stigma" of setting aside the picture of what your writing and publishing dream looked like when you first started. You aren't alone if you're already walking along the road of self-publishing, equipped with information and advice that seems to work for everyone but you.

Being a writer is the best thing in the world. Even as I'm planning a mid-winter vacation, I can't imagine not writing for the entire length of my time "off". I write every day of the week with periodic days off, but that time off always includes writing of some sort, even if it's only taking notes for story ideas.

Getting your work out into the world is difficult and can be discouraging in a way that shatters your soul. I hope this book encouraged you. Check out the recommended reading. And if you're one of the ones who can't let go of that dream of a book contract from New York City, why not publish a short story or a collection of stories or a novella and see what happens. You don't even have to use your own name.

Polish your work. Get it edited. Put an ebook out there, and run a small Amazon Ad (detailed instructions). Experiment with putting your book in Kindle Unlimited. See what happens.

I'm glad I self-published because doing so has allowed me to write the stories that interest and move me. It's allowed me to control my schedule and the creative presentation of my books. It's allowed me to make money without handing ownership of my work to a faceless entity for the rest of my life.

As I sit here today, the possibility of making more money than I ever would with a small publishing contract is within sight. The chance to support my husband and me as a fiction writer is a blurry vision on the horizon that's growing more clear every day.

CHANGING COURSE

Inkubator

I published this book in late December 2018. As so often happens in life, as if the forces of the universe are toying with us, my writing career changed dramatically a few weeks later. In January 2019, I was approached by a small, innovative crime fiction publisher.

Inkubator Books had seen an ad for one of my novels, read the book, and thought despite my characterization of my work as Suburban Noir, the story fit nicely into the psychological thriller genre. Irony abounds.

The timing of their arrival in my life struck me in another way. Over the New Year holiday, I'd been browsing in a bookstore, looking for books about craft. I announced to my husband that since marketing my work was making me insane, I wanted to devote 2019 to improving my craft. Of course we would still advertise my novels and do whatever we could to increase their visibility, but I needed to dial down the intensity of my focus on that frustrating pursuit.

I wanted to fall back in love with writing. I didn't want to rest on the positive reader feedback I'd enjoyed. I wanted to craft even more life-like characters and tell ever more immersive and gripping stories.

Inkubator Books is unique in that they invest a lot of time into developmental editing to ensure books fit the expectations of readers in the genres they publish.

Their concept of a writer's room—taken from the television approach of a writers' room to develop scripts—is not utilized by any other publisher I'm aware of. Because I'd vowed to improve my craft, it seemed as if they'd stepped into my career at precisely the right moment, ready to help me up my game.

The other reason I signed with them was because they focus on the power of the Amazon algorithms to connect readers with books, utilizing Kindle Unlimited and Amazon's advertising tools.

Working with the co-founders has been fun, full of creative energy, and mind-boggling as I've watched their finely-tuned book launches drive my novels to a level of sales I hadn't come close to on my own.

I don't have a moment's regret that I self-published. I consider myself a hybrid writer now because Inkubator Books is fully supportive of any work I want to publish on my own. I've continued writing my serial killer series and have plans for a historical psychological thriller trilogy, possibly with ghosts!

I still firmly believe that acquiring and working with an agent in the hopes of getting a contract with one of the Big Five publishers is fraught with pitfalls. I would still have very serious doubts about licensing my copyright to an international corporation where I'd be swallowed like a guppy.

Inkubator Books gives hands-on attention to each book they publish and every writer they work with. Their contracts do not consume the rights to my work for the rest of my life. There are no draconian grabs for control of my ideas and subsidiary rights. They invite my input regarding pricing, cover design, blurb composition, and title choice.

What I'm saying, is that working with this small group of people still gives me all the things I've loved about self-publishing, but does the heavy lifting (all the lifting) for marketing.

Every writer's path is different, and mine has led me to this place.

They are a dream to work with and they have been a huge factor in making my dreams come true. I am now making a living as a fiction writer.

Recommended Reading

All of these books had a huge impact on how I write, how I think about the writing life. All come highly recommended. I've read all of them more than once.

On Writing, Stephen King (does any list of writers' resources not include this book?)
Writing Down the Bones, Natalie Goldberg
Immediate Fiction, Jerry Cleaver
The War of Art, Stephen Pressfield
Turning Pro, Stephen Pressfield
Fearless Writing, William Kenower
The 90-Day Novel, Alan Watt
The Irresistible Novel: How to Craft an Extraordinary Story That Engages Readers from Start to Finish, Jeff Gerke
Bird By Bird, Anne Lamott
A Newbies Guide to Publishing, Joe Konrath's blog (read the archives starting in 2010)

My obsession with unlikable characters and their place in the world continues. If you're drawn to "unlikable" character, there's a lot of meat in these articles.

Lionel Shriver (We Need to Talk About Kevin) —
Perfectly Flawed: In defense of unlikable characters

Claire Messud (The Woman Upstairs) — *What Kind of Question Is that?*

Roxanne Gay (Difficult Women) — *Not Here To Make Friends*

Kelly Braffet (Save Yourself) — *Quit Talking About Likable Characters*

Andrew DeYoung — *Why We'll Never Stop Arguing About Likable Characters*

About the Author

Cathryn Grant is the author of Suburban Noir novels, the Alexandra Mallory series, the Haunted Ship Trilogy, the Madison Keith Ghost story series, and short fiction. Her writing has been described as "making the mundane menacing".

She's passionate about fiction that explores the shadows of suburban life and the dark corners of the human mind, believing that the human psyche is, as they say in Star Trek — the final frontier — a place that we'll never fully understand. She's fascinated by characters who are damaged, neurotic, and obsessed.

Cathryn's fiction has appeared in Alfred Hitchcock, Ellery Queen Mystery Magazines, Shroud Quarterly Review, and anthologized in The Best of Every Day Fiction and "You, Me & A Bit of We" from Chuffed Buff Books. Her short story, "I Was Young Once" received an honorable mention in the 2007 Zoetrope All-story Short Fiction contest.

She wrote this book to give inspiration to writers considering self-publishing (or doubting their choice), to let them know what it's really like, that they're not crazy to self publish, and they can do it if they have passion and perseverance.

"By keeping quiet I was being selfish. There are people everywhere struggling to get businesses off the ground. Others shared their stories of failure and success." —Kathy Ireland

When she's not writing, Cathryn reads and tries to play golf without hitting her ball in the sand or the water. Find out more or contact her through her website at CathrynGrant.com

www.ingramcontent.com/pod-product-compliance
Lightning Source LLC
LaVergne TN
LVHW041213080426
835508LV00011B/934